HEADS YOU WIN

An Easy
Guide to
Better
Headline
and Caption
Writing

By
Paul
LaRocque

Library of Congress Cataloging-in-Publication Data

LaRocque, Paul, 1931-
  Heads you win : an easy guide to better headline and
caption writing.
     p. cm.
Includes index.
  ISBN 0-9729937-0-3
  1. Newspapers--Headlines. 2. Photograph captions. I.
Title.
  PN4784.H4L37 2003
  808'.06607--dc21

                                    2003008596

Copyright © 2003 by Paul R. LaRocque

Bulk purchase discounts are available for corporate
training programs. Please call Ed Avis at toll-free 866-
443-7987 for more information.

ISBN 0-9729937-0-3
Printed in U.S.A.
Printing 10 9 8 7 6 5 4 3 2

Marion Street Press, Inc.
PO Box 2249
Oak Park, IL 60304
708-445-8330
www.marionstreetpress.com

The headline is the most concise of all nonfiction writing forms, the copy editor's haiku. LaRocque reminds us, again and again, of its power to engage, or, when done badly, to repel. We need this book.
ROY PETER CLARK, SENIOR SCHOLAR, POYNTER INSTITUTE

Which headline is worse? The dry-as-paint-flakes line about the unnamed panel passing the unidentified plan, or the double entendre about laid priests that leaves readers howling over their morning paper? Paul LaRocque tells us how to avoid both in a book that is as full of wit as it is of wisdom.
JUNE KRONHOLZ, REPORTER, WALL STREET JOURNAL

Paul LaRocque uses laughter to leverage learning. Humorous headlines come from real life and readers learn from the way the author skillfully dissects each of these headlines.
LARRY L. ROSE, PUBLISHER, CORPUS CHRISTI CALLER-TIMES

The headline is a publication's bridge to its readers, and LaRocque's advice can help keep that bridge in good repair.
PHILIP SEIB, PROFESSOR OF JOURNALISM, MARQUETTE UNIVERSITY

Great headline writers think in headlines. They imagine events and the headlines that go with them. And they write cutlines about the accompanying photos. They put out newspapers in their minds. That's what Paul LaRocque prepares us to do with this excellent book.
DAVID MCHAM, PROFESSOR, UNIVERSITY OF HOUSTON

ALSO BY PAUL LAROCQUE:

THE CONCISE GUIDE TO COPY EDITING
PREPARING WRITTEN WORK FOR READERS
(MARION STREET PRESS, INC. 2003)

ORDER AT WWW.MARIONSTREETPRESS.COM

For Paula

Contents

Introduction

This book is intended to help those writers and editors who love words and labor to produce headlines and captions that sell stories and enhance pictures in the media, whether newspapers, magazines, newsletters, or electronic. Headlines are usually the first words readers see on a page, whether it's printed on paper or on a screen. A good headline stops readers and leads them into the story. A poor headline may be passed over and the story below, no matter how interesting, ignored. A good headline not only catches reader attention, it informs readers and urges them to read on.

Captions help pictures tell their story. A good caption enhances the value of a picture, while a poor caption diminishes the photo's value.

The headlines and captions in this book are mostly from newspapers. Most of them were published just as they appear in this book. A few headlines I created or modified to illustrate a point. The type faces are different from the originals, of course. It would be chaotic to attempt to reproduce the faces used by various publications in the original headlines and captions. And in most cases, I have used a down style simply for reading ease. Down style is the normal sentence style — capitalizing the first letter of the first word of the headline and any proper nouns. However, I have used original style — capitalizing the first letter of each word or capitalizing all the letters in the headline — to illustrate particular problems.

Most of these headlines I collected during my many years as a journalist and journalism educator. I and my wife, Paula, have used them in our lectures and workshops on writing and editing. Many of the headlines are humorous because they contain errors or double entendres. I use them in this book to catch your attention, to illustrate how not to write headlines, and to help you avoid writing laughable headlines. But most of all, this book is intended to be a quick, handy guide to better headline and caption writing. Some of the headlines have appeared on the famous back page of *CJR* called "The Lower Case." A few came from *AJR*'s monthly feature "Take 2."

As a newspaper copy editor, I always thought the most exciting part of each editing task was writing the headline. Producing a good headline — one that "sings" — can be as exhilarating as flying an airplane, biting into a chunk of chocolate cheesecake, or hearing a great line in a movie or play.

To be a good headline writer, you must love words. I fell in love with words in elementary and high school in Worcester, Mass., where the Sisters of Mercy and Sisters of St. Joseph orders taught and encouraged good writing. My first headlines were on a hand-written underground newspaper I produced in the seventh grade, published only when I was in the mood. Later, I wrote headlines for publications across the country — in the Marine Corps, in college, in public relations work, and at several daily newspapers, all the time enjoying the word play that goes into headline writing. I wrote a lot of heads of which I was proud, some that were just OK, and a few stinkers. Love of words, I learned, does not guarantee sparkling headlines, but it helps headline writers maintain a favorable success average.

I am also indebted to many tutors, editors, and friends who throughout my career have praised and rejected many of my headlines. My wife, Paula, has been one of my most helpful and toughest critics. Her suggestions and encouragement have been invaluable. Colleagues and friends who have inspired and critiqued my work are too numerous to list here. But one deserves special mention: Richard Leonard, my editor when I was on the rim of the state desk at *The Milwaukee Journal*. It was a great day on the state desk when one of our headlines sailed through Dick. Many he kept and rewrote. It made us work harder, hoping with each story to get a headline past Dick.

I've passed on my enthusiasm for headline writing to

those who would listen in newsrooms, classrooms and workshops, using the methods detailed in this book. For the most part, I have used a how-not-to-do-it approach to headline writing, a method I borrowed from wordsmith and journalism teacher John B. Bremner. He used that approach in his headline book *HTK*, which I have used many times over several decades of teaching headline writing. Besides showing you how not to write headlines, the errors of headline writers past provide a light touch — some humor to lighten the learning. Headline writing is a serious business, but a sense of humor can help headline writers keep calm when the editor is shouting, "I need that headline now!" And there are times when a good sense of humor is essential to turning out a catchy headline pun or metaphor that sells a story.

The title of Bremner's book, *HTK*, stands for "hed to kum," trade jargon meant to tell printers that the headline will be written later. There's a story that has been passed down to generations of journalists and printers about a prankster's play on *HTK*. In the days of hot metal type, stories were written on copy paper and sent to the print shop by pneumatic tubes, much like the tubes at a drive-in bank. The newsroom prankster wrapped a beheaded fish in copy paper, marked it *HTK*, and sent it through the tube to the printers. The story is probably apocryphal because I've heard it from several sources in several slightly different versions. But it's fun and shows that people who work with words have a sense of humor and are not dullards.

As you will see in this book, headline English can be crazy: Nouns sometimes appear to be verbs or adjectives, and verbs imply unusual actions. Have fun reading this book, and don't make the same mistakes that are illustrated here. Above all, be careful, write winning heads, and don't lose yours.

Chapter One

Silly heads

The cautious seldom err.

— Confucius

Headline writing can be fun — both for the writers and the readers. Journalism publications regularly reprint headlines that went awry, and Tonight Show host Jay Leno has put together several books on headline bloopers. *The Milwaukee Journal-Sentinel* copy desk has a scrapbook of headline and other newspaper goofs collected over several decades.

Whether it's a double-entendre headline, a malapropism or spoonerism, goofs in print or speech are entertaining. They usually were not meant to entertain, but because of some cerebral short circuit, the words missed their mark. Words are the building blocks of language, and when the blocks are misplaced or misused, what is said sometimes is not what is meant. A public figure says he'll reduce government by *nutrition* instead of *attrition*. A radio announcer says *cool tit* instead of *tool kit*, and a newspaper headline says *Dolly cancels performances, lays band*. Those were simple mistakes: wrong word, spoonerism, and dropped word (*off*). It's easy to do — if you aren't careful.

Dropped words are but one of many causes of headline bloopers. Failure to consider a word's multiple meanings can be just as fatal as an omission for the writer/editor and just as hilarious for the reader: *Married priests in Catholic church a long time coming*. The headline writer and editor failed to see that *coming* can be interpreted in more than one way — to the delight of readers. Have a "dirty" mind when writing headlines — it's safer.

Obviously, the writers of those headlines did not intend to produce laughter. They meant to provide information — to sell stories. Something interfered. Headline writers generally have a pretty good idea what they want to say, but they often have to overcome several obstacles, such as space, type size, time, and limits on their own abilities — vocabulary, imagination, creativity, and knowledge of the language.

Space is a major problem, especially in newspapers — making all the essential information fit a tiny space can be difficult. For example, a newspaper design editor assigns a one-column headline in large type on a complex story about congressional committee action on foreign aid. So the headline writer comes up with something like this:

Panel acts on aid plan

Good headlines do two things:
- They capture reader interest.
- They capture the essence of the story.

Panel acts on aid plan does neither. How many readers would that headline attract? It's flat and packed with headlinese. A curious reader with nothing better to do might read part of the story, perhaps just the lead, to see what action the panel took on what aid plan. The headline has no emotion and almost no action. The action, *acts*, is abstract. In fact, the entire headline is abstract. Did the panel approve or kill the plan? And what panel? What aid?

Good headlines need room to speak. Design editors

should consider that when assigning a headline. And headline writers should speak up and negotiate when design editors give them an impossible task. All should be thinking of the readers.

With that headline, readers have no idea of the nature of the panel and thus no interest in its action. And they have no idea how its action affects them, if at all. There is no hint (essence) as to the nature of the aid plan. In short, the headline is merely a few words stacked in two layers. And worse, the words are headline clichés — *panel, acts, aid,* and *plan.* They are short words and usually fit — and they are overworked, particularly on stories dealing with government. They're so overused that readers largely ignore them.

Headlines, like stories, should employ fresh words and conversational language. How would you react if a friend greeted you with, "The panel acted on the aid plan"? You'd probably run off shouting over your shoulder that you were late for a meeting. Think of headlines as conversation openers. They should stop readers and make them read the story.

Sometimes a headline may capture reader interest, but the story beneath it seems unrelated. The headline may be incorrect, misleading, too cute, or unintentionally funny. The headline writer may have good intentions, but the head doesn't come out the way it is intended — it doesn't match the story. Good headlines come from clear and careful thinking. What do you suppose the writers (and editors) were thinking when they produced the following headline:

**Postal union head says humans
should replace bulk systems**

The headline is trying to say that the union wants the post office to use people instead of machines to process mail. But the headline writer failed to see the double meaning. What was written was not what was meant. The story is about people and machines, not gastro-intestinal transplants. And consider this headline:

**Severed leg follows
victim after accident**

Yes, the leg did follow the victim, but in a vehicle. The picture this headline creates is of an accident victim hopping down the road and a leg hopping along behind him — an image one might get in a Stephen King novel, but not in a media report on an accident.

The next headline could ruin a breakfast:

Here's how you can lick Doberman's leg sores

Ugh! Obviously, the headline writer meant *lick* as a synonym for *control*. *Lick* is several letters shorter. It *can* be a synonym for *control* or *overcome*, but this headline suggests something disgusting — especially for breakfast reading. Perhaps when a longer word, such as *control*, didn't fit, the headline writer might have sought a shorter word from a thesaurus. A thesaurus or synonym finder can be a valuable tool for headline writers, but writers should realize that all the synonyms listed for a word will not work in all contexts. If a word doesn't seem to fit, cross-check synonyms until you find a word that fits and is appropriate.

The next headline seems innocent, but it has a fuzzy image.

Utah girl does well in dog shows

The confusing combination of *girl* and *dog* in this headline leaves too much to reader imagination. Yes, the girl does well in the shows, but it is her dog that wins the prizes. If you don't want a blooper head, you have to weigh each word and its relationship to the others in the headline.

The consequences of failing to look at words closely can be amplified by certain headline styles:

**Textron Inc. Makes Offer
To Screw Co. Stockholders**

It's obvious that this headline writer didn't mean that stockholders were being propositioned. It just happens that in the abbreviated company name (American Screw Company), *screw* can be read as a verb. It's also unfortunate that the headline style is upper case — beginning each word with a capital letter. Had the publication employed a down style — *Textron Inc. makes offer to Screw Co. stockholders* — there would be less chance for misinterpretation.

English offers many opportunities for a "two-faced head" — one with a double meaning. Read headlines aloud before sending them to production. Sometimes hearing the headline will uncover a second and unintended meaning. Let a colleague read your headline, especially when you've had a difficult time writing it.

All those headlines were published, as were most of the examples used in this book. The segments in Chapter 3 will illustrate particular headline-writing headaches. Bloopers are fun and can be aspirin for the aching headline writer's pain. So, enjoy the mistakes of others, and learn from them.

Chapter 2

Getting started

Sentimentally I am disposed to harmony; but
organically I am incapable of a tune.
— Charles Lamb

Writing headlines is something like writing a song: The words must be appealing and in harmony with the music. And a headline must "sing" — that is, it must be in harmony with the story and "sound" pleasing to the reader. Of course, headlines usually are not read aloud, but they resound in the head and make mental noise — the slam of a gavel, blare of a trumpet, tinkle of a wind chime, or a joyous burst of laughter. "Singing" headlines set the mood for the story, making readers sit up and take notice of important news or information or relax and enjoy an entertaining feature.

Within those moods are two major types of headlines — lookers and hookers. Most headlines are lookers. They simply tell readers what's in the story. Those stories are routine and straight, and readers usually are drawn to them by their interest in the story topic — a sensational crime, significant government action, important information, or heavy drama. The hookers are headlines that grab readers by the shoulders and say, "Read me, I'm interesting." They usually appear on stories that are not routine — feature stories, think pieces, personal columns, opinion articles, etc. Hooker headlines often merely offer a hint of what the story is about, teasing readers with cleverly worded information. Whether a story calls for a looker or a hooker, the headline usually should not tell the whole story. It should provide essential information that raises enough interest to draw readers into the story.

This is a looker:

**China arrests U.S. writer
on charges of espionage**

This is a hooker:

**What happens when
King Alan goes?**

Both headlines catch reader attention. Readers want to know who and why in the China arrest, and they want to know what will happen when Greenspan leaves government. Because "King Alan" is in a headline over a financial column, few readers will ask, "Who's Alan?" But even if they did, you've still got a hooker in that question, "Who's King Alan?"

Hooker headlines are usually not questions. Mostly they imply a question. Here's a hooker on a feature about French film director Michael Haneke:

A different kind of shock treatment

That headline invites readers to ask, "What is the different shock treatment?" And they have to read the story to find out.

Occasionally a hooker head can work on a routine story. And sometimes a looker can be perfectly fine atop a feature story. Be flexible. Follow guidelines rather than rules. The main guideline for good headline writing is a question: Does it work? Headline rules are fine for establishing consistency — type, style, etc. But publications should rid themselves of silly headline rules that restrict creativity, readability, and interest. Style and type rules should be sensible and flexible. Remember, a headline is written for readers, not for editors and designers. Keep readers in mind always. And look for fresh words that will excite and entice readers. Why — if the words fit — would a headline writer use *hot* when *searing* or *fiery* means more? Avoid stale headlinese such as *hit, rap, panel,* etc. And don't parrot the lead of the story or needlessly borrow words from the text. Read the entire story, and rely on its focus for headline material.

Sometimes headline writers have a clear picture of the story, but the headline ends up out of focus. So headline writers blame space and time restrictions — "I would have written a better head if I had the time or space." No matter the medium — newspaper, magazine, newsletter, book, online, etc. — headline writers will face restrictions. Below are a few simple steps that will help harried headline writers overcome those restrictions and produce headlines that sing. This exercise may seem to take too much time when time is nowhere to be found, particularly in the rush to meet a deadline. But it's such an easy drill that most head writers can do it quickly and subconsciously during the headline-writing process. And it's an exercise that headline writers may need only when writer's block strikes. If you use it a few times on paper or on your screen, you'll find that the process comes to you subconsciously when you're planning a headline.

Remember that this formula is not the only way to write a headline. It's meant as stimulant, something to fall back on when you are stuck or to get beginning headline writers started. As you write more headlines, you'll perhaps develop variations of this formula or an entirely different formula. The important points to take from this exercise are focusing on the whole story and finding the right words — strong words that fit. It's also important that you find a system that works well for you. If you are writing winning headlines and you have an entirely different formula, stick to it. As the saying goes, if it's not broken, don't fix it.

This two-step exercise emphasizes the looker headline. It can be used to write a hooker head, and a few paragraphs at the end of the exercise illustrate how the formula can be adapted. You'll get an entirely different approach in another exercise following this one.

Here is the first story. Write a one-column, 24-point headline in three lines (the steps will follow):

Virgin Retail Group, a unit of closely held London-based Virgin Group Ltd., said it is negotiating to open a minimum of 10 major multiplex theaters in the U.S. during the next three years.

Virgin, which recently opened a 75,000 square-foot music/video/software store In New York's Times Square, currently operates 24 multiplex cinemas in the United Kingdom.

Ian Duffel, president and chief executive of Virgin Retail Group, said each of the multiplex theaters will probably have more than 16 screens, and will feature digital sound and perhaps private boxes. In addition, certain of the multiplexes will be developed in conjunction with a Virgin megastore. "Right now we're negotiating to open two of those complexes in New York City," said Mr. Duffel, who declined to identify the proposed neighborhoods. Virgin previously announced plans to open 30 of its Megastores by 2000, including five in Manhattan.

Mr. Duffel said Virgin Retail has funded its current growth internally, but that it may turn to the public markets in the future to bankroll its proposed centers. Virgin Retail, based in Los Angeles, currently operates six stores in the U.S., including five in California.

(From *The Wall Street Journal*)

1. After you've read the whole story, write a short active-voice sentence that best describes the story's focus. As you read the story, make note of or mark some key words. First find action words. In this story you might note *open*, *expand*, *develop*, *grow*, *plan*, and *propose*.

Then find key nouns. Here are some: *Virgin Retail Group*, *London*, *theaters*, *United States*, *stores*, *screens*, *United Kingdom*, *megastores*, *multiplexes*.

Now, you're ready to find the main action word in the story. Is it *plan*? It could be, but is there a stronger, more precise action word? What about *develop*? Let's try it and see how it works in writing a focus sentence. Ask who is developing what.

Virgin Retail Group will develop 10 multiplex theaters. Stop there. You can see *develop* is not working. It's not right for the context. Try *expand*. *Virgin Retail Group will expand its U.S. holdings.* That's better, but you don't have *theaters* in the sentence. You must add a few more words:

> Britain's Virgin Retail Group will expand its U.S. holdings in the next three years to include at least 10 multiplex theaters.

Obviously, that sentence won't fit in the assigned space, type size, and number of lines — one column, 24 points, and three lines. But it will give you something with which to start. Write it in the blank space above the story on your screen or on a piece of paper, whatever is convenient. Now you have a focus and information — the most important steps in writing a strong headline. Here's your next step:

2. In a 24-point, one-column, three-line head, perhaps you can fit about 12 units on each line, a unit being one full space. Some letters, such as *i* and *l* use only a half space. Others such as *m* and *w* use one and one-half spaces. The counts used in the exercise below are approximate. Unit counts vary with type styles. It's good to keep

those values in mind when drafting a headline, even though the computer will do the final counting for you. Again, pick out the essentials, this time from the summary sentence — **Virgin, expand, theaters**. Note that you have in those three words the skeleton of an active-voice sentence — subject, verb, and object. Now ask yourself what other information is important to the story. Numbers? Location? Try a headline that gives readers the most information. It may not fit, but it's a start. Keep revising your headline until you get one that fits and gives readers as much information as possible. Here's a beginning:

Virgin to expand (14)
U.S. holdings (11.5)
to include theaters (15.5)

That's not going to fit. How far off is it? Line one is too long. Two is within limits, only a half unit short, and three is too long. Also, you want to avoid *Virgin* because it can create a two-faced head. Let's try again.

British firm (10)
may expand (10)
U.S. holdings (11.5)

It fits, but you lose theaters. Perhaps you need to change some of the information or the action. Try synonyms. See what can be deleted without harming the message.

British retailer (13)
may open 10 (10.5)
U.S. theaters (11.5)

It's almost a perfect fit, and it says most of what you want to say. You may have to squeeze the first line a bit to make it fit. And you can bend the guidelines a bit to split the second and third lines — something you can do in one-column, multi-line heads. You have covered the essentials: Subject, **British retailer**; verb, **may open**; object, **10 U.S. theaters** — a complete thought that leaves out only the time (in the next three years), information that is secondary and which readers can find early in the story. Note that you gave up *expand* in favor of *may open*. Using *retailer* instead of *firm*, along with *10 theaters*, implies expansion, not only of business but also into another area.

Let's take a different approach. You are asked to write a feature headline on the same story. For example, imagine you are writing for a publication that deals lightly with most headlines — the entertainment magazine *Variety*, for example. Try to create something clever or exciting that says the essentials. You can use the same information from your focus sentence. It has all the essentials, but it's heavy. Step out of your heavy shoes and get into dancing slippers. How about this:

The British are coming to your neighborhood theater.

Like it? Okay, now make it fit. You can write:

Brits are coming (14.5)
to your (6)
local theater (10.5)

Way out of balance. Instead of coming, let's try this:

British plan (10)
U.S. invasion (11.5)
via big screen (12)

Now you have a light (hooker) headline using practically the same method that you used in the straight (looker) headline. The focus is the same, but you played with the headline words, giving up the action word *expand* in favor of *invade*, which takes you into the land of metaphor.

Next, let's try an entirely different type of story and a different approach to headline writing. Almost any accurate headline would attract if the story is bizarre. You don't have to struggle to write it, but you can have fun. It's the kind of story headline writers dream of. The page designer has given us room to be innovative and clever. The head is three columns wide. The top line is 36 points and has a maximum count of 24, but less would be better because the line will be centered. The bottom line is 18 points, also centered, with a maximum count of 48, and it can be full. Here's the story:

FORT COLLINS — A Fort Collins entrepreneur whose doughnut shop will feature topless waitresses has found no opposition at the Larimer County Board of Adjustment and will go ahead with sneak preview plans this weekend.

The adjustment board on Tuesday night refused to place a roadblock in front of Dennis Cortese's attempts to open his controversial establishment.

The five-member board failed to muster the four votes needed to require Cortese to go through a special review to open Debbie Duz Donuts.

The special review would have determined whether the topless doughnut business adheres to zoning regulations.

Barbara Trevarton, manager of a mobile home park near the controversial doughnut shop, filed an interpretation appeal in late June, saying that Cortese's business was a place of entertainment, not a restaurant, which is an allowable use.

An entertainment business is not allowed without a special review from the county. The board voted 3-2 against Trevarton's request.

Cortese said his plans for a sneak preview of his business are still scheduled for Saturday and Sunday.

Joseph Fonfara, lawyer for Trevarton, told the board that because Cortese's business featured nudity and higher prices on coffee and doughnuts that Debbie Duz Donuts was an entertainment establishment, not a restaurant.

(From The Associated Press)

It's another business story, but it obviously cries for a clever headline — a hooker. The story is offbeat, light, and has elements of conflict and humor. It's a story that challenges your sense of humor and wordplay.

So, let's take a different approach. You don't have to analyze this article to determine its focus. It's obvious — fun. The headline must capture the mood of the story, which is offbeat and light, and it must be clever, inviting, and have a touch of conflict. It might be a label headline.

Forget the active voice diagram you set up in the first exercise on British theaters. Concentrate on words. Here are some of the words you have to play with: *topless*, *doughnuts*, *Debbie Duz Donuts*, *sneak preview*, *breasts*, *boobs*, *bra*, *chest*, *coffee*, *dunk*, *hole*, *dough*, *dozen*, *taste*, etc. You get the idea. Think of words that you can associate with a topless doughnut shop. Let your mind soar, or perhaps plunge to the depths of poor taste.

Instead of an active-voice sentence, come up with a catchy phrase for the top line. Pretend that you are on Madison Avenue writing ad copy. You might come up with some words that are not in good taste, but jot them down anyway. You're thinking. The words may not be printable, but they'll give you ideas that perhaps you can work into something that is printable — it's a kind of stream-of-consciousness formula. Let's try it. And don't worry about fitting at this point. That will come later. Here's a start:

Waitress, there's a boob in my coffee

That will never sail, but it's fun to write. It's also too long.

Doughnuts have toppings but waitresses don't

Maybe, but it's also too long. And it's a bit dull, lacking rhythm and mood.

This ain't Krispy Kreme

I like it. It may work for a top line. It's short, conversational, and catchy.

Not your mom's donut shoppe?

It's OK, but a bit too long and not "krisp."

Thanks for the mammaries

Clever, but perhaps too risqué and it reaches a bit. However, a good deck to that top would be *But I'll just have a plain doughnut and coffee*. I like it, if the editor will accept *mammaries*. It has another drawback, though — the news value, government approval, is missing. It's an entertaining headline, but remember you're writing a headline on a *news* feature.

Let's try the Krispy Kreme head. Now let's get to the deck and a news link — government approval. You have plenty of room. How about this:

Topless doughnut shop gets OK to hold sneak preview

The finished work is both newsy and entertaining, and it fits — the top line counts 20.5 and the bottom 46.

This ain't Krispy Kreme
Topless doughnut shop gets OK to hold sneak preview

That stream-of-consciousness method works best on light stories. Hard news and complex stories need more precision in planning a headline — a looker head. The hooker head relies more on cleverness than information, and it only has to give readers the essence of the story. You have room for entertainment — both your own and the readers'.

Personally, I like the stream-of-consciousness approach because it's pleasure rather than work. Compare it to a fitness routine. If you work out regularly, are in shape, and you feel good after a long jog or a bike ride, the routine is enjoyable. If you have just had knee surgery and the rehabilitation includes a routine of dull legwork, you don't enjoy it. It's boring, but you realize that you have to do it if you are going to get back to the exercises you enjoy. Likewise, you may not always enjoy the two-step analysis approach to writing a headline, but sometimes it's necessary to keep fit.

Regardless of the routine you follow to produce good headlines, there's always pleasure in seeing your creation in print. Headline writers don't get bylines, so readers won't be singing your praises as they do for the star writers on your staff. You'll never hear a reader say, "Another great headline by Joe Schwartz." But you will know you wrote a winner. And sometimes, you'll hear a writer say, "Great head, Joe. That really made my story."

I always envied the editors on weeklies and small dailies because they did everything — wrote the stories, designed the pages, wrote the headlines, took the pictures, and wrote the captions, and sometimes even set the type and put it in the pages. And everyone in town knew that they did it. I have captured a bit of that small-town intimacy in recent years by publishing the newsletter for my homeowners' association. I do it all — stories, pictures, design, and write the headlines — the task I enjoy most. I get comments from neighbors when I walk the dogs, "Good newsletter, Paul."

But I'm afraid association members are like most readers: They enjoy the stories and take the headlines for granted. Headline writing on most publications of any size is a mostly thankless job. You get satisfaction in knowing you've written a good head, but acclaim is rare. If your publication enters your headlines in a contest and they win, that's great. But that comes only a few times a year.

Headline writing is a labor of love. It's love of words and the enjoyment of working and playing with them. Good headline writers have wide knowledge, read a lot, enjoy word puzzles and games, and puns. They aren't nerds with green eyeshades and sleeve garters — a stereotype from old newspaper movies. They are men and women with quick minds who love the English language and enjoy using it so that others can enjoy it, too. The best headline writers, I believe, are born with the talent but others can develop with practice and discipline.

The next chapter deals with specific headline-writing problems. The topics are categorized and alphabetized, making them easy to find when tackling knotty headline-writing problems. Remember, these are guidelines and not rules. Here's the most important question to remember as you write, whether you are writing headlines, captions, or complete stories: Does it work? And you can make headlines work by carefully reading the story before you begin and by using strong, simple words. Always look at a headline task through reader eyes. Ask yourself, "What would attract me to this story?" Usually, your first idea will be the best. Too much thought about a headline sometimes can lead to fuzzy heads that evoke a reader "Huh?" instead of "Wow!" Your goal as a headline writer is to aim for the "Wow!"

Chapter 3

Headline mechanics

A powerful agent is the right word. Whenever we come upon one of those intensely right words in a book or a newspaper the resulting effect is physical as well as spiritual, and electrically prompt.
— Mark Twain

This chapter deals with the nuts and bolts of headline writing — the devices that fasten words tightly so they don't fall apart when the eye picks them off the page. We'll look at headlines that didn't work and examine the reasons for their failure. And we'll discuss why some headlines worked well. Keep in mind that whether the headline is off-beat or straight, its primary goal is clarity. This chapter has four sections:

• Section 1 deals with form, the basics of headline writing such as being accurate, precise, and concise.

• Section 2 suggests ways headline writers can attract readers with figures of speech and other devices, and it shows what happens when such devices are not used carefully.

• Section 3 examines language traps and how headline writers can avoid them.

• Section 4 deals with sensitive issues that confront head-

line writers — libel, fairness, objectivity, double entendres, etc.

Section 1 — Form

Nothing irritates readers more than a headline that
misleads or confuses. Therefore, headline writers must
carefully consider the impact of each word, number, and
fact — and its placement in a headline. Headlines can't
afford to be almost accurate. They can't be vague. They
can't be ugly. They must capture both reader attention and
the essence of the story over which they preside.

Here are some points to consider when striving to
write crisp, clear headlines.

■ Accuracy

Always read the whole story carefully before writing a
headline. That may seem like a given, but the rush to meet
a deadline sometimes can override that common-sense
guideline. It shouldn't. Read the story. Send the headline
along later if you have to. Also, check your headline for
spelling, accuracy, sense, etc., before sending it. Don't
rely on the next editor to fix the things you missed, and
don't rely on spellcheck. You have primary responsibility.
Spellcheck is fine. Use it, but do so with caution.
Spellcheck can catch some spelling errors, but it cannot
help you if you used *their* instead of *there* or *hear* instead
of *here*. Let's look at a few headline problems that could
have been avoided by careful checking.

Polish singer wins Nobel Prize

That headline appeared on a story about Isaac
Bashevis Singer, a Polish-born writer who won the Nobel
Prize for literature. But Singer isn't a singer. The headline
writer apparently just glanced at a few words in the lead

and wrote the head. Read the whole story, and read it carefully.

Sunny, cold tonight

Obviously, the writer meant to say that it would be sunny today and cold tonight, but probably ran out of space. The result: a headline that makes the sun shine at night and therefore makes no sense — unless you're writing about the Arctic, which was not the case. A simple fix: *Sunny and colder*.

AIDS researchers fear
heterosexual epidemic

Think. Read the headline aloud. Do researchers really fear that there will be an epidemic of heterosexuals? Go back to the basics and rebuild the headline. The headline is active voice. It has a strong verb — *fear*. *AIDS* and *heterosexual* are essential elements. What can go or change? Perhaps a synonym will help. How about this?

Researchers fear spread
of heterosexual AIDS

Researchers fear epidemic will not fit in the top line. *Researchers fear spread* will. *Spread* is not as strong as *epidemic*, but it will work. You then move *AIDS* to the bottom line. The headline fits, and it makes sense.

■ Alphabet soup

It seems that no matter where we look today, we see acronyms and initial abbreviations — FBI, CIA, NCAA, NAACP, NATO, OPEC, etc. Those are some of the more familiar servings of "alphabet soup" that pop up regularly in headlines. The guideline for abbreviations and acronyms is go easy. A headline full of capital-letter abbreviations is hard on the eyes, and the brain. Here's an example:

PCLOC's 30th
G&S a tribute
to D.E.C.

Hmm! What does it mean? On to the next story.

A wise headline writer came up with this headline as a comment on alphabet soup heads. The writer used abbreviations of two government agencies to make a point about abbreviations in headlines.

You CETA words, but they have NOAA meaning

If you must use acronyms and abbreviations use them sparingly and with caution. Use the ones readers will understand, but don't overdo it. One to a headline is enough, unless you absolutely need two. It could happen that you have to write a head on a story in which NATO and OPEC are key players, or the FBI and CIA. Remember, these are guidelines, and the most important factors in writing headlines are capturing reader attention and telling the story. Don't sacrifice those elements to adhere to a guideline such as limiting headlines to one abbreviation or acronym. Use common sense.

In the headline below, the initials of the Pasadena Independent School District can have a whole new meaning.

Summer ends for 36,000 PISD kids

As can the abbreviation of Metropolitan Utility District.

Two people report
man in MUD guise

Beware of the guys in a mud guise.

■ Appearance

A good headline not only fits in the allotted space, it fits the story. That is, it is the right type size, face, mood, and tone. For example, you would not usually write a light headline on an obituary. But you can. The death of a comedian might warrant a humorous but tasteful headline.

Type face can add to a headline's effectiveness. Type faces have personalities. Most roman type faces, such as Times or Times New Roman, are serious and businesslike. Bold type is more serious and dramatic. Heavy sans serif type is ominous:

PRESIDENT DECLARES WAR

All-capital-letter headlines are difficult to read. Italic type is casual and not as businesslike as the upright faces. It suggests movement with its slight leaning to the right. (I once worked for an editor who would not allow italic type on any serious story. The copy desk crew interpreted his unwritten rule as "italic is funny.") Italic type can be used for variety. If the headline is roman, an italic deck makes the type display more attractive. Italic also can be used to emphasize a word or phrase in a headline. And all-italic headlines can bring visual relief among a page of roman headlines. A good headline writer will be familiar with type faces and styles. Books on type should be part of the headline writer's library. Type experts may vary in interpreting the moods of type, but knowing what they say and using your own common sense can help you pick a type that is right for your story when those special occasions arise.

Beware, however, of too much variety. The occasions for stepping outside your publication's type styles should be few and infrequent. All publications have style rules or guidelines. Guidelines are best, because they are not rigid. A publication's style manual may specify that headlines be written in specific type faces. However, style guidelines should not forbid deviations when the occasions arise, especially when feature articles beg for something different to attract readers. For example, Nadianne type has a formal feminine face that could be used in a headline display over a feature about the etiquette of table setting. Old English Text could be used on a story about book publication in the 16th century. Stage Coach might go well with a story on the old West.

Playing with type can be fun, but the purpose of the headline should not be forgotten — to attract readers. Above all else, the headline must be easy to read. Size, face, and mood must yield to readability.

Type size today is flexible. It can be manipulated to help a headline fit in a tight space. Computers have given headline writers great freedom in fitting headlines. A quick touch of the keyboard and a headline can be squeezed to fit by merely reducing the type size a fraction of a point or changing the spacing between letters. Slight adjustments are fine, and readers will not notice. Major adjustments in type size and spacing, however, should not be made without the consent of the page designer.

■ Clichés

Headlines easily attract clichés. Because headline writers have so little space and so few words to make a point, they sometimes resort to headlinese — words such as *nix*, *nip*, *rap*, *hit*, *panel*, *plan*, etc. Avoid them if you can. Try for fresh language in headlines. If you're stuck, ask the design editor for more space. Tight one-column headlines breed clichés.

This headline appeared in *Variety*, an entertainment publication known for its wild headlines that often contain clichés. It headed a story on a farm-life movie that was not popular in rural areas. Fine for *Variety*, but perhaps not for some other media.

Sticks nix hick pix

■ Cuteness

Headline writers always should be clever, but cleverness should not produce headlines that are too cute. Always remember that your job as a headline writer is to attract readers quickly and easily. If readers have to decipher a headline, they may just skip your story and go to the crossword puzzle. The writer of this head was clever, but perhaps a bit too clever. It was written for a story about Arkansas lawmakers abandoning efforts to pass legislation that would require warning labels on music that may have hidden messages recorded in reverse. The headline writer captured the mood of the story, but perhaps not many readers because most don't want to take time to figure things out. (Hold it up to a mirror for translation.)

llib no pu evig srekamwal sasnakrA

■ Labels

Label headlines have no action, so sometimes they can be weak. But some label heads imply action and are strong enough without verbs to attract readers. The next headline appears to have action, but it doesn't. It's not only a weak label headline; it's confusing because its words can be nouns or verbs, or even adjectives. Readers have several choices: Did a dump murder a suspect? Of course not. Did someone dump someone suspected of murders? Perhaps. But readers must go to the headline deck to get the important clue.

Dump murders suspect
Georgia holds
ex-area man

The headline appeared over a story about a man being arrested in the deaths of two women whose bodies were found in a dump. The main headline, which is supposed to be adjective (*dump*), adjective (*murders*), noun (*suspect*) — a label headline — is not only a bad label, but a bad headline.

Label headlines can be inviting, however. They usually need a deck to help them, but not always. Here are a few that stand alone and are strong. They tell a story and imply action. Often they appear on opinion pages.

The price of occupation

That headline topped a *New York Times* op-ed piece about Israel's occupation of the West Bank, Gaza, etc. The headline provokes curiosity, "What is the price of occupation?" and leads readers into the column to find the answer.

Twenty years of AIDS in America

That headline is clear, strong and comprehensive. You could struggle to find a verb for that headline, but it would be a waste of time. The label works fine on that *Wall Street Journal* section-front story on AIDS.

Ballet review
Evening of memories, balloons and surprises

This headline has no verb, but the action is implied. An overline tells readers that it's a ballet review, and the headline gives a strong hint of the action. The words *memories*, *balloons*, and *surprises* create visions of a gala evening and entice readers to join the festive spirit. A verb in this head and a more conventional treatment might even dim those visions. This version below is all right, but it lacks the imagination of the verbless headline — too many words blur the vision:

Ballet produces evening of memories, surprises

Feeding off others
**Plagiarists abound
in a cut-and-paste
environment**

That headline appeared in an art display on a section front of *The Dallas Morning News*. The story was about plagiarism online, and the art (shown above) was several fish feeding on illuminated light bulbs (symbols of ideas). Clever art, clever headline.

■ Numbers

Unnecessary numbers clog headlines. Use only numbers that are important to the understanding of the headline. If a story is about a disaster toll, statistics, spending, or an athletic contest, numbers may be important to the headline. Use them, but don't use too many. And don't use them when they are not essential to the headline, as is the case in this padded head:

Pet-dog, 3, bites its
master, 35, to death

Some numbers have double or off-color meanings (No. 1, No. 2, 666, and 69) and generally should be avoided. For example, a colleague once wrote a headline that contained the number 69 and was surprised that the headline was rejected. The desk editor explained 69 and why the headline was inappropriate. After that, whenever my colleague considered using a number in a headline, she would ask, "Is that a dirty number?"

■ Obvious

Don't state the obvious. Headline space is too precious to waste. Here are a few heads that probably left readers scratching their heads.

Study: Dead patients usually not saved

Women make the best moms

**Food is basic
to student diet**

**Blind woman gets new kidney
from dad she hasn't seen in years**

■ Padding

Avoid excess words. A headline is too important and has too little space to include words that do not do any work. Don't add a word just to fill out a line. If you come up short, rewrite the headline, making it stronger. You may be able to tell readers more about the story. Or, if the headline is short and strong, leave it alone if your style permits a bit of white space. White space is better than wasted words. Don't add *is* or *are* or *a, an,* or *the* to a headline unless it improves readability — makes it clearer or gives the head rhythm. Most of the time, forms of the verb *to be* and the articles *a*, *an*, or *the* can be left out of headlines. Here's an example of *are* being necessary. The headline makes no sense without *are*. (See the section on Verbs, p. 54, for more examples.)

You are what you eat

A Canadian editor told me that his newspaper hired quite a few British copy editors, and they had a habit of adding *now* to headlines to make them fill out a line. That's deliberate padding, but sometimes headline writers pad unconsciously. For example, when writing a headline for a fatal accident, do you really need to say, *3 people die in head-on crash*? The word *people* is padding. A news editor I worked for would toss those "people" headlines back to us with the comment: "Of course it was people. It wasn't monkeys." We headline writers waited for the day when monkeys were involved in an auto accident so that we could write *3 monkeys die in head-on crash*. Of course, it never happened.

■ Parroting

Don't parrot the lead of the story. Find the story focus, and try to capture the whole story and not just what the lead says. Writers work hard to develop good leads. It's lazy and hurtful to copy the author's words in the headline. It's also not good to copy phrases from the story's body except when the phrase — perhaps a quotation — is so strong that it will attract and hold readers. President Richard Nixon's famous 1973 quotation, "I'm not a crook," made headlines across the country. And well it should have.

■ Questions and quotes

Questions and quotes in headlines can be inviting,

but they can also become a crutch for deadline-pressured headline writers. Use them when they work. If a question provokes curiosity and compels readers to get into the story, fine. If an answer is obvious, forget it. If a quotation does a better job of selling a story than anything else you can create, it is right for the story. If it's just picking up a phrase from a story, forget it. (See the section on Parroting, p. 36.)

The question headline below works. It's compelling. Readers want to know what in the boss' past caused bad behavior.

**Is the awful behavior
of some bad bosses
rooted in their past?**

The headline below picks up a phrase from a story about a man with an artificial heart. However, the quotation is appropriate and strong, and it does not parrot the lead. It invites readers to find out how "life is wonderful," a quotation from the patient.

**'Life is wonderful' for the man
with a self-contained artificial heart**

■ Splits

Headlines should be easy to read. Splitting parts of verbs, modifiers, and other word groupings on separate lines usually makes difficult reading. The eye and mind should see each line as a separate unit. Reading only the first line of this head may jolt readers:

**House passes gas
tax on to Senate**

Splits are not always misleading or difficult to read. But generally, it's good to avoid them. In the headline above, *gas* modifies *tax*, and the two words should be presented as a unit: *gas tax*. Don't split verb parts such as *has gone*, or adverb and verb such as *votes swiftly*. Avoid splitting prepositions and objects such as *for payment* or *in committee*.

Some splits are not difficult to read and may be acceptable. When splits come in the middle of a multi-line headline, they can be acceptable, especially when a three-line head is a tight count, such as you'd get in a one-column, 30-point head or a two-column, 60-point headline. However, good planning will avoid such predicaments. Page planners, whether they are writing the headlines themselves or passing the task on to a copy editor, should keep in mind the story theme and any problems a tight count will present in writing the head. Best of all, try to avoid those tight two- or three-line heads. They seldom are inviting.

The best way to deal with splits is to use common sense. Read it aloud. If it doesn't sound right, fix it. This split is ridiculous. It splits the number 11.

**Chamber
salutes 1
1 firms**

Below is an example of a split in the middle of a multi-line headline. The lines are so short that the reading flow is vertical, and the eye can manage a split with no harm to readability. In reading one-column headlines, the eye moves vertically instead of horizontally, making splits easier to read.

**Insurers
fined for
payment
delays**

■ Style

It is important to have style guides for headline writing. Most publications use a harmonious set of type faces, set limits on white space, etc. Style is meant to give a publication identity as well as make it uniform, attractive, and readable. Therefore, it should be crafted carefully so that it does not work against those goals. For example, an "up" style — capitalizing each word of a headline except prepositions — may be attractive, but it can eat up valuable headline space. Capital letters are wider than lower case letters. If your publication freely uses one-column headlines, you may want to consider using a "down" style, capitalizing only the first word of the head and proper nouns.

■ Time element
(See also Tense)

The time element is usually not a factor in headline writing. When the action occurred is usually left to details in the story. What happened is more selling than when it happened. However, on those occasions when the time is included in the headline, the tense of the verb should agree with the time.

Section 2 — Figures of speech and other devices

Good headline writers love words, and they love to play with them — to tickle readers with an amusing pun, make headlines come alive with a clever metaphor, or delight readers' ears with ringing onomatopoeia. Figures of speech can make headlines sing, but they must be used with care. When forced, those devices can sound a sour note. Here are some examples of word devices that work — and some that don't.

■ Alliteration

A smart bit of headline alliteration can perk up an otherwise dull topic. This news headline from about 70 years ago appeared on a story about U.S. Sen. Reed Smoot's fight against pornography.

Smoot smites smut

■ Metaphors

The metaphor headline can brighten your publication's page, even when used on straight news stories. The story does not have to be "light" to carry a "light" headline. The keys to success in using a clever headline are taste and mood. Even though you are playing with words, you must be fair, accurate, and tasteful. Here's a headline on a story about IBM's woes in producing software called Office Vision, which gives executives access to any computer in their companies. Both the main headline and deck employ successful metaphors — *black eye* and *stumbles*.

A black eye for Big Blue
IBM stumbles on Office Vision

The following metaphor on a food story, however, goes too far along the food chain to make it work. The result is confusion. Are we writing about beef or poultry?

Grilling turns flank steak from ugly duckling into swan

Make just a few changes, keeping in the beef line, and you have a "tasty" and attractive headline: *Grilling elevates lowly flank steak to filet mignon status.*

■ Onomatopoeia
(See also Metaphors, Play on words, Words)

Words that derive from sounds can add pleasure to headline reading, sometimes giving them life. Words such as *smack*, *plop*, *buzz*, *clunk*, etc., not only provide sound to your headlines, they provide visual action. Readers can almost hear a book *plopped* on a table or a crowd *buzzing* with excitement. Here's a sports headline that makes good use of onomatopoeic words:

Once again, Oilers
knocking, pinging

The headline writer plays with echoic words — *knocking* and *pinging* — that are often associated with poor performance of an automobile engine. Of course, the Houston Oilers football team is not knocking and pinging. Oil is a necessary ingredient of smooth engine operation — without pings and knocks. Word play makes that headline roar. It's much more apt to catch readers than a bland *Once again, Oilers aren't doing well.*

■ Play on words
(See also Metaphors, Onomatopoeia, Words)

If you love words, you'll love writing headlines. The headline writer has wonderful opportunities to play with words. Writing a headline is like playing Scrabble — you don't get bonus points, but you get readers with your winning words. Writing a headline that makes readers smile as well as informs them can be as satisfying as a gourmet meal, without the calories. Again, beware of going too far. Overwriting is as bad as overeating. A cute head can easily become a monster if the headline writer carelessly uses words or is not attentive to taste. Here's one that the writer, playing with crappie, the name of a panfish, perhaps did not read aloud:

Caught a' crappin'
46-inch muskie landed on a panfish line

But playing with words made this headline sing:

**Yodel
lady
who?
Woman fulfills
fantasy at opry**

The headline writer cleverly used the sound of words — the sounds made by a yodeler — to entice readers into a story about a woman who is a court bailiff during the week and a yodeler on weekends.

■ Puns
(See also Play on words, Rhythm and rhyming)

Puns are fun, but they must be logical. Use them sparingly. You'll know when it's time to pun. The headline idea will jump at you. Never force a pun. It should be natural, easy to read, and entertaining. And be careful that you don't produce an unintended pun (see Sounds). The writer of the following headline perhaps did not intend a pun.

Wife gets snippy over vasectomy refusal

The pun below obviously was intended. It was over a story about sheep cloning.

Ewe look a little familiar

Also intended was this pun on a story about a museum and visitor center at the site of a meteor crater:

A hole new way to view crater

■ Rhythm and rhyming

(See also Alliteration)

A headline that rhymes or has rhythm can be as pleasing as music. Or it can grate like a chalk squeak on a blackboard. Again, reading your work aloud should tell you if the headline works. Here are some headlines that have rhythm:

A storm
in Norman
OU campus is abuzz
over harassment charge

The top of the headline plays on the rhyming label for Desert Storm commander Gen. Norman Schwarzkopf — Stormin' Norman. And it fits the situation — a fuss over harassment charges at Oklahoma University, which is in Norman.

The great skate

That headline topped a feature about Wayne Gretzky, one of professional hockey's great stars. The rhyme is an added attraction that pleases the ear.

And then there's that famous headline from entertainment magazine *Variety*, which was noted earlier. It's cliché-ridden, but it certainly has rhythm.

Sticks nix hick pix

■ Sound

(See also Onomatopoeia, Puns, Rhythm and rhyming)

Pay attention to the sound of words as well as their meaning. If you don't read a headline aloud, you may miss an unintended sound. This headline on an astronomical discovery seems innocent — until you listen to it. These headlines are in the no-pun-intended category.

Scientists find rings around Uranus

And listen to this one, too.

Columnist gets urologist in trouble with his peers

Section 3 - Language traps

Headlines, like sentences, should be clear, easy to read, and informative. Generally, they should follow English rules and guidelines. However, sometimes headline writers may play with words, break or bend a rule, but they must play carefully. Clarity is your goal, so when tempted to break a language rule or guideline, first consider the consequences. As we saw above, confusion is sometimes the result of cute word play. Keep this principle in mind: Know and understand the rules of language before you attempt to break them. Here are some suggestions to help headline writers avoid the many pitfalls of the English language.

■ Active voice
(See also Passive voice)

The active voice is the best choice for headlines. It's natural. It's the way we speak: *He hit the ball.* Not: *The ball was hit by him.* We use active-voice sentences in the body of a story because they are stronger and shorter. In headlines, however, sometimes passive voice is preferred because the words fit better or because the actor is unknown or unimportant.

■ Attribution

(See also Punctuation)

Attribution is essential in headlines that need it. It's needed to avoid opinion in a headline on strictly objective stories. Subjective material, such as editorials, op-ed columns and personal columns, often does not need attribution in headlines. The material is opinion and the headline can generally stand without attribution. In this headline, attribution tells readers that a study has provided evidence that surgery has been a more successful treatment for epilepsy than drugs. It's not proven. It's merely the conclusion of a study. Thus, attribution is needed.

**Study says
surgery
tops drugs
in epilepsy**

In the headline below, the source of the accusation is not named, but readers know that Nebraska is accused of unequal use of the death penalty — *is said to use* — and that it's not a fact.

**Nebraska
is said to use
death penalty
unequally**

The next headline requires no attribution, because it is quoting statistics, something that falls into that broad category of common knowledge.

Gun arrests rise this year in New York

Use of a colon or dash to signify attribution is fairly common in headlines, but it can be confusing and is a lazy way to attribute. (See the section on Punctuation, p.50.)

Here are two confusing headlines that attempt attribution with a colon and a dash:

Cause of AIDS
found — scientists

Silent Teamster gets cruel punishment: lawyer

In the first headline, readers must decide whether scientists cause AIDS or scientists are saying they have found the cause of AIDS. In the second, is the lawyer the cruel punishment or is the lawyer saying the punishment is cruel?

■ Grammar

The rules of grammar are the same for headlines as they are for the body of the story. An incorrect preposition, for example, can change the meaning of a headline:

Three men charged
for abuse of girls

The preposition *for* in that headline implies that the men paid something for the abuse. In fact, they face criminal charges. Replace *for* with *in*.

In the next headline, the writer may have been trying to be cute and to capture the mood of a story about the intelligence of young Americans. It may work, but the writer is gambling that readers will see the play on words and not think the newspaper *be getting stupider*.

Are young
Americans
be getting
stupider?

In addition to a good dictionary and thesaurus, headline writers should have handy grammar and usage books. A grammatical error in a headline is far more visible than an error in the body of a story. Look up words when you are unsure of meaning, spelling, usage, or syntax.

■ Misspelling
(See also Accuracy, Typos)

Few things can be more embarrassing to a publication than misspelling a word in a headline. Misspellings are bad enough in text, but a headline in large type amplifies the error. It shouts to readers, "See how careless we are." Misspellings, whether in text or headlines, damage the credibility of a publication. Check twice or more before releasing a headline to publication. A computer spellcheck is a good start, but don't rely on electronic checking. Computers check spelling, not how a word is used. They do not tell you that you should use *too* instead of *to* or *diary* instead of *dairy*. If your typo happens to spell a word that's in the computer's dictionary, that word won't be flagged.

Here are a few examples of some embarrassing mis spellings:

Viet official's twin
tells why he defecated

Obviously, the author of this headline meant *defected*.

Museums utilizing TV to attack visitors

TV is the scapegoat for many social problems, but it can hardly be charged with attacking museum visitors. It should have been *attract*. (*Utilizing* instead of *use* is padding. See the section on Padding, p. 35.)

■ Modifiers

Watch where you place words because they may turn

on you. Stacking prepositional phrases can cause problems for headline writers and readers. Reading aloud (I know, I've said it before) helps you detect misplaced modifiers before readers do. Be careful to place words and phrases next to the words they modify. Here are some misplaced modifiers that give readers the wrong impression:

Bronx man leaps to his death before officers arrest him

So police read him his rights as he lay splattered on the sidewalk? No. Try this approach: *Bronx man leaps to death before officers can arrest him.*

27 flying to see pope die in Mexico crash

The 27 people were not going to see the pope die in a plane crash. They died, the pope lived. Turn the headline around, insert a stronger active-voice verb, and the headline avoids the misplaced modifier: *Mexico crash kills 27 flying to see pope.*

■ Passive voice

(See also Active voice, Punctuation, Two-faced head)

The passive voice is sometimes unattractive in headlines. There is nothing *wrong* with the passive voice. It's just not as strong as the active voice. And we don't talk in the passive voice. Active voice is shorter, stronger, and natural. We say, *Barry hit the ball.* We don't say, *The ball was hit by Barry.* Active voice is subject, verb, object — actor, action, receiver. Passive voice is object, verb, subject — receiver, action, actor. Sometimes passive voice may not have an actor because the actor is understood or not important: *Sen. Clump was arrested.* Police, the actor, is understood and not essential in that sentence. Who was arrested is more important than who did the arresting. Headline construction has the added problem of space to contend with, so passive voice sometimes is preferred, because it fits, because the actor is not important or is unknown, or because more can be said. Here's an example:

Police arrest mayor

Mayor jailed in fight

There is nothing wrong with the first headline. It will catch reader attention, and it tells the essentials — the mayor has been arrested. That's a story that will attract readers. However, the second headline, a passive voice head, tells readers more — that the mayor was arrested in a fight. Here's an example of a passive headline that fits better than the active-voice head:

Passive:

Island hit
by floods,
landslides

Active:

Floods,
landslides
hit island

Both headlines say the same thing, but the passive headline has balance and no white space. If your headline style is to make each line balance or come as close to balancing as possible, the passive headline would be preferable.

Passive voice is also acceptable when the actor is not known, as in this headline:

Minister slain in church

The actor is unknown, and it would be awkward to force an active-voice headline on this story, unless other important elements were known and important to the story.

■ Punctuation

Use punctuation in headlines only when absolutely necessary. Punctuation slows readers, and headlines are meant for speed reading. Periods usually aren't used in headlines. For a full stop between words, use a semicolon. That is, use it if necessary, but try to avoid a full stop in a headline. Likewise, use question marks and dashes only when necessary. Use the colon when it links two equal parts — a fact and explanation, for example — but avoid using it for attribution. A colon normally needs more than just a name before it to introduce a quote in text. A headline is no different. You would not write in your text, *Bush: read my lips*. You would write, *Bush says read my lips*. In addition, colon heads can be confusing. Quotation marks generally should be avoided in headlines. If you must use a direct quotation, place it in single quotation marks.

Here's colon headline that's confusing:

Reagan: a peril
too close to home

That headline leaves readers wondering whether Reagan is the "peril." The headline writer used the colon to indicate attribution. Reagan is speaking about a peril; he is not the peril, as the headline suggests.

One of the uses of the colon is to connect a fact with an explanation. In this headline, the colon is used to help the reader connect two items, fear and data — one explaining the other.

Behind fears
of trucks
from Mexico:
shaky data

Of course, you can argue that the colon is a space saver, and you use it only when you don't have room for "says." That's a poor excuse. With a little effort, a good headline writer can include the attribution without a colon.

Let's look at a colon headline and see what you can do to improve it. This headline appeared on a story in which Homeland Security Director Tom Ridge tells governors they will have ample input in a new national terrorism alert system. The headline:

Ridge: Governors will have
a say in terror-alert system

There is plenty of room in that headline for full attribution. No need for the colon. In fact you can make the headline stronger by substituting *promises* for the weaker *will have*. How about this:

Ridge promises governors
a say in terror-alert system

The next headline is ambiguous because it lacks punctuation.

Reader is upset over
dog eating Filipinos

The reader is not upset because a dog is eating Filipinos, but because Filipinos are eating dogs. *Dog eating* is a compound modifier and needs a hyphen for clarity — *dog-eating Filipinos*.

Here are some brief guidelines for punctuation in headlines:

- Period - Avoid except when needed in abbreviations.
- Comma - Use sparingly when needed to join two independent clauses or to set off appositives.
- Semicolon - Use instead of a period for a full stop.
- Colon - Don't use for attribution.
- Quotation marks - Avoid but when needed use single quotation marks.
- Question mark - Generally avoid questions, but when appropriate, use it.
- Exclamation mark - Avoid it. Most exclamations do not need a mark to identify them as such.
- Parentheses - Avoid them. They are visually awkward and hinder readability.
- Hyphen - Use when needed — to join compound modifiers, for example.
- Dash - Do not use for attribution.
- Ellipsis points - Generally avoid them.

■ Tense

(See also Grammar)

Headlines generally are written in the present tense to imply immediacy, but that guideline should give way to common sense and correct grammar when a time element appears in a head. This headline is ungrammatical:

Michael Irvin surrenders
to police Saturday night

To be correct, the tense of the verb has to change to past — surrendered — because the action is clearly in the past. Also, is the time essential to the headline? In rare cases, it is. In this case, it is not. It's merely padding. Keep it simple. Save some space: *Irvin surrenders to police*.

■ Typographical errors
(See also Misspelling, Accuracy)

Writers and editors used to blame typographical errors, or typos, on the printers. Today, when computers have done away with most rekeyboarding by "back shop" personnel, the fault for the typo lies mostly with the originator — the writer or editor who created the headline. However, doing away with second-hand typesetting has not done away with the typo. Here are a few obvious (and humorous) typos, some of which probably were made by printers. See if you can solve the mystery of this headline. How did it happen?

Herd of Exotic Atroyed at Sea
Will Not Be Desfrica Beasts

Yes, parts of the top and bottom line were transposed. Somehow, each line became two pieces, either in the typesetting process or in the cut-and-paste work by the printers. In haste to meet deadline, the last part of each line was transposed. The headline should have read, Herd of Exotic Africa Beasts Will Not Be Destroyed at Sea.

This next headline was squeezed a bit too much. See if you find the missing space.

Thompson's penis a sword
Governor poised to break
own record in budget vetoes

Just one little typo — one letter — completely changed this woman climber's ambition. And perhaps Mr. Everest's, too.

Would she climb to top
of Mr. Everest again? Absolutely!

Sometimes, a word left out can be just as dangerous as

the wrong word. Guess which word was omitted in this headline.

Three found slain in Pizza

If you guessed *Hut*, you're correct.

Or one letter too many.

Actor reveals he's AAA member

It's hardly worth revealing that you're a member of the American Automobile Association. Perhaps Alcoholics Anonymous (AA)?

■ Verbs

Headline writers sometimes begin a head with a verb, dropping the subject — the assumption being that the subject is readily understood and thus not needed. For example:

Fight order
to ban book

Don't assume readers will supply the missing subject. Good headlines should not make work for readers. They should help readers. They should be clear, concise, inviting, and informative. That usually means including subject and verb.

However, sometimes the *verb* can be dropped from a headline because it is understood. For example, forms of the verb *to be* are often left out of headlines without any damage to meaning. And in tight situations, valuable space is saved. For example, if you were writing this as text, you would use *is* before *likely*, linking the subject *county* with its modifier *likely*. In a headline you can drop *is* with no loss of meaning:

**County likely to help
fund Olympic vote**

Also, when a form of *to be* is used as an auxiliary verb, it can often be dropped with no effect on meaning.

**Insurers
fined for
payment
delays**

In that case, the headline writer faced a tight count, about seven units per line, and *are fined* would not fit. The headline is perfectly clear without *are* — and it fits.

Section 4 - Sensitivity

Above all, headline writers must be sensitive. An offended reader is often a lost reader. Word meaning is not absolute. Word position often governs meaning, and words with multiple interpretations should be carefully considered. Avoid headline structures that can produce a double entendre. Avoid offensive words, and always avoid words that are potentially libelous. Courts have found that headlines alone can libel. Here are some suggestions for the sensitive headline writer.

■ Ambiguity
(See also Two-faced heads)

Sometimes what seems like the right word for a headline may not be. That's why it is so important to give your headline a careful reading — aloud is best — before putting it in print. Ask a colleague to read it, too. Two heads are better than one (no pun intended). Context must be considered. Here are a few examples of "right words" used in contexts that make them ambiguous, and quite funny.

Robert Bork disrobes to take on critics

Yes, Bork disrobed. He stepped out of his judicial role to respond to critics. The headline writer had the "right" word, but it was the wrong word for this headline. No, Bork did not flash or moon his critics.

Attack from rear can be hairy

That headline introduced a feature column in which a woman lost her wig when her car was struck in the rear by another car. When you play with words in a headline, it helps to examine your headline in a different color — an off-color. Your readers will. Save yourself from embarrassment; read your work with an "off-color" eye, and you won't end up, as this writer did, with a hairy rear.

Defendant's speech ends in long sentence

Pay special attention to words that have multiple meanings. The defendant's speech has sentences, and courts pronounce sentences. A sentence can be words or time. In this headline the word is ambiguous. The headline writer considered only one meaning, and readers, considering another, got an unintended chuckle.

Asbestos suit pressed

Press is a useful headline verb. It's short and it's strong. But it has more than one meaning — to try to influence by insistent argument, to apply pressure, to iron clothing, etc. *Suit*, too, has more than one meaning, so we arrive at the unintentional humor of ironing an asbestos suit. (At least it will not burn.)

Babies are what the mother eats

Are and other forms of the verb *to be* are often left out of headlines. They are short connecting or auxiliary verbs, and headline writers can often omit them with no loss of meaning. (See the sections on Verbs, p. 54, and Padding, p. 35.) In the headline above, *are* is needed to make sense. *Babies what the mother eats* is a fragment, and it doesn't make sense. The *are* in that sentence is meant to connect to two equals, such as in the saying, "You are what you eat." *Are* works fine in that sentence. There is no room for misinterpretation — your body is a reflection of your diet. The headline writer meant to say, *Babies reflect what the mother eats*, or *Mother's diet affects babies*. But the writer instead apparently chose to play off the well-known saying "You are what you eat." The "right word" wasn't right. Result: mothers eating babies.

Chains popular
as bridal gifts

There are chains and there are chains. In this headline, of course, the writer meant the kind of chain that is worn as jewelry, not the type used for restraint. Beware of the double entendre.

Panda mating fails,
veterinarian takes over

Here is an unthinking juxtaposition of two independent clauses, bringing into question the role of the veterinarian in panda reproduction. Obviously, the vet is not going to mate with the panda. But that's what the head suggests. (See the section on Punctuation, p. 50, for the role of the comma in headlines.)

The careful headline writer will consider all meanings before sending a headline to publication. Read your head aloud. Hearing what you have written perhaps will help you discover that the "right word" you have chosen is actually not the right word. The two-faced headline may entertain your readers, but that's not your intention.

Again, a thesaurus or synonym finder can be a helpful tool for headline writers, but should be used with caution. Not every word listed as a synonym will work in every context. For example, you will find that *sort*, *combine* and *group* are synonyms for *mate*, but you could not substitute any of those words for *mate* in the first line of the panda headline. These won't work: *panda sorting fails*, *panda combining fails*, *panda grouping fails*. Those synonyms have similar meanings, but the context governs their use.

■ Body parts

There's all sorts of slang for body parts. Good headline writers should educate themselves in the slang (mentionable and unmentionable) of body parts. Only through familiarity can you avoid slips like the head below.

Beaver chase leads to bust

But this headline from Great Britain, about Michael Foot, a member of Parliament, who is heading a group concerned with nuclear disarmament, makes good use of body parts to have a bit of fun with a routine bureaucratic appointment. Some editors might think it goes a bit too far, but it's good clean fun.

Foot heads arms body

■ Fairness

(See also Taste)

Don't distort. Headlines are supposed to attract readers, but if the headline reaches for a minor point merely to sell the story, the headline writer is being unfair to the story's author, the subject of the story, and readers. Here's an example: A biography about a person who has devoted his life to helping the poor contains deep in its body a quote from the person saying he once spent the night in a jail because he was arrested for being drunk and disorderly. The rest of the story dwells on his good works and his motivation. The jail time had no influence on his avocation, but is merely a candid and interesting anecdote passed on by the subject. The headline writer comes up with this:

Good Samaritan spent night in jail

An interesting and provocative headline. It teases the reader, but it is unfair to the author and to the story's subject. Find something else interesting, something that tells the whole story, and not just an anecdote that is beside the point of the story.

■ Juxtaposition

Juxtaposing words or thoughts without consideration of alternative interpretations can result in headline snickers. In this headline, the word *stiff* is unfortunately used with *funeral*.

Stiff opposition expected to casketless funeral plan

In the next head, the hugging and AIDS death are not related, but placing them in the same sentence (headline), unfortunately causes readers to wonder.

Boy hugged by pope
dies of AIDS at 7

The pope hugging a boy who is seriously ill is a human-interest story. And he becomes *the boy who was hugged by the pope* for the remainder of his life. So when the boy dies, the story recalls his being hugged by the pope. The relationship must be handled carefully if it is used in the headline, or perhaps it is better not to deal with that angle in the headline. This revision leaves out the hugging:

AIDS finally claims
boy who met pope

The way to avoid such embarrassment is again to read the headline aloud.

■ Libel

In a broad sense, libel is written or oral publication of material that maliciously damages a person's reputation. Specific legal definitions of libel vary from state to state, but the general concept — published defamation — is universal. Every headline writer's library should include material on the legal aspects of publishing, particularly something dealing with libel. The Associated Press Stylebook has an easy-to-read section on media law, including libel.

The important thing for headline writers to remember is that a headline alone can be libelous, regardless of what the story says. Readers might never get past a headline, and libel plaintiffs are always willing to call in experts to testify to that. A correct story under a libelous headline may be of little or no help to the defendant in a libel suit. So, avoid overstating the case in the headline, and of course, don't be cute at the expense of the truth. Avoid words and expressions that can lead to libel suits — words that can be considered damaging to reputation. Attribution won't help. If the words are libelous, attributing them to the source will not get you or your publication off the hook. The next section considers some loaded words that could be libelous.

■ Loaded words

Some words should sound an alarm when they pop up in a headline writer's thoughts — words that imply intolerance, lying, cheating, criminal actions, a loathsome disease, membership in an organization that is in disrepute, etc. Here are but a few words that should send up a red flag:

adultery	drunkard	Nazi
AIDS	fraud	pimp
blackmail	gambler	scam
bribery	hypocrite	villain
coward	illegal	whore
crook	mobster	
drug dealer	murderer	

The list could fill pages. It's not necessary to have a list of "red flag" words. Common sense should tell a headline writer when a word is potentially defamatory. And if you have doubt about a word, don't use it. Consult an editor and/or an attorney. There are defenses in libel action — truth, fair comment, testimony in court, public figure, etc. — but it's best not to make a judgment regarding privilege based on limited legal knowledge. Let an expert decide. You may win the libel case in court, but you will have spent a great deal of your publication's money doing it. The goal is not to be sued, and if you are sued, the legal hassle should be worth the price and effort. In any case, let someone in a higher and more knowledgeable position decide on whether to publish a headline that may be libelous. And remember, attribution does not get a publication off the hook. Police may have called the person a crook, but if it is not true, the medium that publishes the defamation is just as liable as the police officer who said it.

■ Names

Proper nouns can be tricky, especially when your headline style is upper case — capitalizing each word of the headline, or writing the heads in all capital letters. A name may seem quite innocent to the headline writer, until it is placed in context. *Bill* is a word that may be a proper noun — a person's name — or a piece of legislation, financial statement, or an advertisement. Here's an example of *bill* gone awry:

**Farmer
Bill Dies
In House**

A farmer named Bill did not die. A piece of legislation dealing with farmers died. The headline perhaps would not be misleading if the style were lower case — capitalizing only the first word and proper nouns.

The headline below confuses colors and names, despite being lower case. It appeared on a story about a black political group withdrawing its endorsement of a public official, whose name is Brown.

Black group withdraws Brown support

The problem is obvious in this headline on a story about a Marlboro, Mass., man:

Cancer society honors Marlboro man

And in Illinois there are communities with names such as Normal and Oblong. Thus, this headline:

Normal Man Marries Oblong Woman

And this from Minnesota:

Fertile Woman Dies in Climax

There's also a Climax in Michigan. When I worked for newspapers in Lansing and Battle Creek, Mich., our headlines concerning Climax, a small town just southwest of Battle Creek, always had to be written with care. We had to be wary, as well, of Hell and Paradise, also towns in Michigan. And there's a Climax in Texas, which also has Cut and Shoot, Dime Box, and Ding Dong (aptly situated in Bell County). Every state has towns whose names can get headline writers in trouble. Be aware of them and be careful. And finally, this headline from a British newspaper:

Little Snoring Man Marries Seething Woman

Avoid using in headlines names of people, places, or things that are not widely known. Good headline writers keep up with current events so that they can judge name recognition. Use common sense. *Smith arrested for burglary* is vague and may get your publication in trouble. Use only names of well-known people, places, and things in headlines.

■ Objective

Unless you are writing a headline on a subjective article, keep opinions out of the head. Don't comment on the news as this headline writer did in a story about government employees taking surplus cheese that was being distributed to the needy.

A lot of rats drawn to giveaway

■ Relationship

Consider the relationship of the words before you write your headline. What may seem perfectly innocent can cause readers to chortle. This seemingly innocent head on new officers of a service club takes on added meaning because of two words — *lions* and *zoo*.

Lions to install officers at zoo

■ Taste

I remember a headline I wrote early in my career. A farmer had suffered a fatal heart attack and fallen into a hog pen where the hogs made a meal of him. A gruesome story. The page layout editor gave me a one-column headline with two lines. The count was 10 units per line. So I wrote, and he accepted:

Hogs chew
dead man

It was on the front of the Sunday paper. Imagine seeing that at breakfast? Ugh.

Sometimes a sensitive story requires tact and imagination to sell it tastefully. This tactful headline appeared on a story about a woman who sued a man who bit her on the buttocks.

He bit hers,
so she sued his

However, the author of the next headline simply tossed good taste aside. The story deals with money paid by large corporations to foreign governments for favorable treatment.

Big business pays millions
for bureaucratic suck

Sometimes even tragic stories contain material that could trivialize a serious act or amuse readers. Tasteful headlines steer clear of such material. Murder is a serious crime, for example, and potentially amusing details of that crime should be dealt with carefully in headlines. Take the headline below. The murder weapon is unusual and is mentioned prominently in the lead of the story — a can of peas. Revealing that weapon in the head may get readers into the story, but it's not fair to the survivors. It's bad enough that relatives of the dead man will have to read about his violent death without others seeming to make light of the murder weapon. Mention the weapon in the story, of course, but not in the headline. And there is also the vagueness of the original headline. How was he killed with a can of peas? Did it fall on him? Did it poison him? *Killed* is vague. *Beaten* is specific.

FW man is killed
with can of peas

A more tasteful and specific headline follows:

FW man beaten
to death at home

■ Two-faced heads
(See also Ambiguity, Words)

The double entendre has embarrassed many well-intentioned headline writers. In the rush to meet deadline or by failing to carefully consider each word, headline writers sometimes provide a laugh rather than information — headlines with double meanings. Most often the ambiguity is caused by words that can be more than one part of speech. This head, for example:

Clinic gives poor free legal help

Is *poor* a noun or an adjective? Obviously, the headline writer meant it to be a noun, meaning the clinic is offering advice to the poor, and not a comment on the quality of the legal advice. A quick reading aloud will tell you that there's something wrong with this head. It's easy to fix: *Poor get free legal help at clinic.* Making *poor* the subject of the headline removes the ambiguity. When you have to revise, go back to the model in Chapter 2. Shift the words around and try substitutes.

Here are a few more two-faced headlines:

Local girl
engaged
to lay pastor

Lay is a verb, and it is also an adjective. Readers asked to make a choice probably would pick the verb interpretation because it caused them to chuckle. This headline is repaired easily: *Local girl, lay pastor are engaged.*

Greeks fine hookers

Is *fine* an adjective or a verb? In that head it's a verb. It's saying that Greeks are imposing a fine on hookers, not commenting on the quality of their prostitutes. *Greek hookers fined.* It's passive voice, but it's not fuzzy. And the count is just about the same.

Girl catcher refuses to wear cup

Catcher is clearly a noun and the subject of this headline. The question facing readers here is not which part of speech it is, but whether the subject is a girl who is a catcher on a baseball team or a person who catches girls. This one needs a complete revision. It's a head that invites writers to play with words. How about: *Catcher says it's not her cup of* . . . The ellipsis points tell readers that the line is not complete, and let the reader fill in the thought — a play on the phrase "not my cup of tea."

The Milwaukee Journal-Sentinel copy desk has kept a scrap book filled with examples of two-faced heads. The office name for the book was "The Dirty Book" because quite often the double meaning was off-color, such as this head from the book:

She carries a man's load

■ Vagueness
(See also Ambiguity)

Headlines should be as specific as they can be and still be attractive. Sometimes a headline can be intentionally vague to provoke reader curiosity. But in most cases, a headline should not be puzzling. Here are some vague heads.

**Baylor employs
fulltime Negro**

The headline topped a story about Baylor University hiring its first fulltime African-American faculty member. The headline is not only vague, it implies that perhaps a person can be a Negro only part time.

Do-it-yourself pregnancy kit to go on sale

An important word is left out of that headline — *test*. Obviously, the kits are not for self-impregnation, as the headline implies. Writing a headline out as a sentence before making it fit your space helps to avoid leaving out key words.

■ Words

This category is a catch-all because words are what we use to write headlines. But because headlines use so few words in attempting to say much, words sometimes play tricks on writers. Reading aloud helps to catch unintended puns, two-faced headlines, and other embarrassing slips. We all laugh at spoken boo boos — malapropisms, spoonerisms, and other slips of the tongue. But headline writers have an advantage: They can read their work before they expose it to their audience. Speakers can do little but blush.

For example, a woman I know well wanted to hear her neighbor's story about the time he had to eject from his navy plane, and she asked, "Tell me about your ejaculation." That same woman, when a waiter bumped her head and apologized with the words, "I'm sorry, I didn't mean to bonk you," said: "That's all right, bonk me anytime."

Here are some mental bonks that should have been ejected by editors:

**NBC abortion stand
arouses clergymen**

Nursing students go the distance

**Home sewers unravel
wardrobe cost mystery**

**Lay position proposed
by bishop for women**

**Marijuana issue
sent to a joint
committee**

Chapter 4

Writing captions

One picture is worth more than ten thousand words.
— Chinese proverb

There is no magic to writing good captions. It just takes a little time and creativity — factors that are sometimes bypassed in the rush to print. Daily newspaper copy editors at an American Press Institute seminar agreed that the biggest problem they faced in caption writing was having to create them in haste on deadline.

Other problems, they said, included:

• Not having enough information about the picture.
• Having either too little or too much caption space to fill.
• Having to write the caption without seeing the picture.
• Being hampered by style restrictions, such as having to use the present tense regardless of the time element in the picture.

Caption writing at too many newspapers seems to be an orphan that no one wants. It may be done by a copy editor, reporter, photographer, design editor, etc. The result is often weak captions. Captions deserve just as much attention as the other elements of a publication. They should be handled with care. Perhaps designating one person or desk to handle captions would have prevented some of the mistakes noted in the next chapter.

In an ideal media world, of course, pictures would be so good and so obvious that they would need only minimal information in a caption. But you are not in an ideal world, and you must make do with pictures that are sometimes confusing and sometimes need a good deal of explanation. The obvious solution to that problem is not to use poor pictures. But when you are faced with a deadline, and the choice is to use the poor picture or fill the space with something else, you probably will publish the picture.

Pictures, like headlines, are art items designed to attract and maintain reader attention. Once a headline captures reader interest, it's up to the story to pick up that interest and carry the reader through the details. And once a picture captures reader interest, it is up to the caption to pick up the interest and complete the picture's story. Few pictures can stand alone. Most need an explanation — the caption.

Captions should adhere to the same guidelines that apply to all written work: They should be clear, concise, precise, and functional. And of course, they should also follow the publication's style guidelines. Those guidelines should be drawn with clarity, brevity, precision, and functionality in mind, and they should be flexible enough to allow creative deviation when the occasion arises.

It is helpful in writing captions to imagine you are writing a voice-over script for television. Imagine the picture you are working with is on a television screen. Let the action speak for itself; there's no need to explain the obvious. You don't hear TV news people saying, "John Smith walks to the jail assisted by Deputy Bobby Joe Jones . . . ." The picture shows what Smith and Jones are doing. The voice tells the viewer why Smith is going to jail. Let the action carry the picture's story. Assist the reader by writing in your caption what is important to the story but not obvious in the picture. But be careful not to go too far. If the picture accompanies a story, let the story provide added detail. Write only enough to help the picture's story and to draw the reader into the story. Some caption writers may ask, "Shouldn't I put more information in the caption for those readers who don't go to the story?" That's a sure way not to get readers into the story. Write captions that are terse and inviting — captions that will make readers want to know more. Sell the story.

If you are writing a "wild" caption for a picture that has no accompanying story, and your caption is going to take up almost as much space as the picture, perhaps you need a separate story. Editors should consider both the picture and the information in both making photo and caption assignments. For example, if the picture assignment is to get workers setting up booths, etc., for the state fair, perhaps a separate story is needed. The caption on such a picture should not have to carry details of the coming fair — dates, prices, events, etc. Create an attractive package of information and art, which includes a terse and attractive caption.

Chapter 5

Caption mechanics

One ought, every day at least, to hear a little song,
read a good poem, see a fine picture, and, if it were
possible, to speak a few reasonable words.
— Johann Wolfgang von Goethe

Captions should "speak" a few reasonable words to amplify the stories told by fine pictures. Here are some guidelines for writing captions. Keep in mind that these are guidelines and not rules. The only rule for caption writing is that the caption must help the reader see the picture as the photographer saw it.

■ Accuracy

Above all, captions should be accurate. If you have several people in a picture, and you intend to name them, make sure you have a name for each. Count the people and your names — and check the spelling of the names, and titles if they are used. It's not only confusing to readers but embarrassing to the publication when names and titles in a caption do not agree with the names in the story.

Insist on seeing the picture before you write a caption. Sometimes in the rush to production, a breaking news photo may still be in the photographer's camera. Wait. Here's what can happen when the caption writer has not seen the photo.

The Associated Press

Effi and Marion Barry leave court for lunch break ... She sat in court without expression watching the FBI's tape of her husband.

The picture shows Marion and Effi kissing, but the caption says, "Effi and Marion Barry leave court for lunch break . . . . She sat in court without expression watching the FBI's tape of her husband."

It's wise to check captions on the page before the page is released to print. Make sure the caption matches the picture. Today's electronic production reduces the odds that a caption will not match. But it can happen. A caption-picture mismatch was more common when pages were built manually. I saw it happen many times. Once, I remember, it happened despite two editors' efforts to correct the error. When checking the first papers off the press, one editor noticed that captions were transposed on two multi-column pictures side-by-side at the top of a page. He ran to the composing room, found the page, and told a printer to switch the captions. Meanwhile, another editor, seeing the same transposition, also ran to the composing room, found a printer (not the same one), and told him to switch the captions. The second editor obviously did not read the captions first — a fatal error. The remade page came out with the same error it had before the changes. The moral: Read before you act. Here's another caption that obviously wasn't checked before being released to print.

BAG DUTY

Carlye Singleton, 4, right, watches her mother, Debbie, and sister, Amanda, 9, use the U-Scan Express to ring up their gro- ceries Wednesday at the Kroger at 5701 W. Pleasant Ridge Road Customers scan and bag items through the self-serve system.

The caption says, "Carlye Singleton, 4, right, watches her mother, Debbie, and sister, Amanda, 9, use the U-Scan Express to ring up groceries Wednesday at the Kroger at 5701 W. Pleasant Ridge Road. Customers scan and bag items through the self-serve system."

That caption obviously was meant for another picture. It names three people, and there are only two in the picture, and the two people are adults, not 4 and 9 years old, as the caption says. The caption writer either was given the wrong picture or the picture was cropped, taking out the two girls. Also, the headline over the picture, *Bag Duty*, is poor taste considering that the picture is of two women. A bad play top and bottom. Check pictures before writing the caption and after the picture and caption are placed in the page.

■ Appearance
(See also Credit lines)

Captions should be attractive. Use a type face that is easy to read. Roman type faces (type with serifs) generally are easier to read than sans serif or italic type. But some sans serif type, such as Arial and Helvetica, are quite readable. Choose a caption type face that fits your overall design — one that is not so much of a change from your body and headline type that it looks out of place. Italic type is fine in short blurbs to emphasize a few words, but it is not easy to read in large blocks.

If you have several lines in a multi-column caption, break the caption into two blocks of type. It is difficult for the eye to track back to the beginning of the next line when there are several lines stacked in a block that is five or more inches wide. One or two lines across wide space causes no problem. But when you have several lines, the eye has difficulty finding the start of the next line when it has to go back across a wide block of type.

When you create two columns of type in a caption, leave an adequate gutter between the blocks — perhaps a full pica or an eighth of an inch. Narrow gutters between blocks can be confusing. Provide enough room to stop the eye from leaping to a line in the second column of type.

All capital or boldface lead-ins are unattractive and disturb caption symmetry. They often are forced, and they sometimes can produce awkward sentences. Headlines over the caption or over the picture are more attractive. Headlines should not clash with the picture. Select headline type faces and sizes carefully, and place them artfully. Be careful that headlines printed over or reversed in the picture proper do not interfere with the picture's story or detract from its artistic and story-telling value. A clever headline can aid the reader's enjoyment of the art. (See *The New York Times* caption in the Mood segment, p. 83.)

Credit lines should be separate from the caption text and should not hinder readability. Place them either between the picture and the caption or beneath the caption. Flush right is a good position in both places. A type face that is lighter or smaller than the caption type is best.

Here's a caption that illustrates some guidelines from the do-and-don't list:

DEPUTIES HONORED — Four of the Wise County Sheriff's Deputies honored at Wise-Jack-Montague Criminal Justice Association's annual banquet on Jan. 23 by the Wise County Sheriff's Department were: (background, back) Investigator of the Year Danny Slimp, (background, front) Rook Ramsey Memorial Patrol Deputy of the Year, Christopher Petty, (foreground, left) Rookie of the Year Christina Hunt and W.A. Hughes Memorial Officer of the Year Debbie Denney.

- **Herald photo by Jane Doe**

The gutter between blocks in that caption is too narrow. Readers can easily become confused, reading across both columns instead of reading down the column. The all-capital lead-in is not attractive and adds little information. The credit line is functional, however. It is smaller and separated from the caption type by type face, size, and placement. The parenthetical inserts to identify people in the picture are confusing and disruptive. With two men and two women in the picture, a simple *left to right* or *front row, back row* would be clearer.

When you have two blocks of type in a caption, it is nice but not necessary to have the blocks even. One block with one more line than the other is preferable to a wordy caption that is padded to make it "fit."

■ Brevity

(See also Wordy)

Keep captions brief. Two sentences usually are enough. The Associated Press formula is to try to keep captions to two sentences, the first describing what the photo shows and the second giving the background.

If background or supplemental information can't be dealt with in a sentence or two, perhaps a separate story or graphic display is needed. The flexibility of modern typesetting allows publication designers great freedom in creating attractive information packages that include photos. Such packages are much more readable than a jam-packed caption.

■ Clarity

Use simple language. A caption should be conversational — terse, clear sentences, usually in the active voice. It should be accurate and easy to read. In that sense, it is no different from any written material. Use common sense. Short active-voice sentences are better because they are conversational. That's the way we talk. Avoid sentences that contain more than one topic, more than three numbers, more than three prepositional phrases, and that rely on jargon or pretentious language.

Here's a caption with an opening sentence that leaves readers scratching their heads.

Like an Hawaiian lei thrown into the sea, Kendall County Junior Livestock Association Directors, including Pat Mattick (aka King Gotta Gut) and Alton Pfeiffer, once again cast pride and dignity to the winds to entertain buyers who support the youth of the county. This year's riotous skit at the annual KCJLA Buyer's Party said aloha to the islands, complete with hula dancers, Don Ho and a two-for-one bride/groom in a Hawaiian wedding.

That first sentence is 43 words, contains a dangling modifier, an ungrammatical *an*, several topics, and creates lots of confusion. The two men in the picture are named, but the explanation of their actions is far from clear. Here's a suggested revision, which in its entirety is only 31 words.

Pat Mattick, left, and Alton Pfeiffer perform in a Hawaiian skit at the Buyer's Party of the Kendall County Junior Livestock Association Directors. The annual event raises funds for county youth.

■ Credit lines
(See also **Appearance**)

Credit lines, which identify the photographer or source of the picture, should be clear, brief, and easy to read, and they should be separate from the body of the caption. Using a different type face, size, or style helps to set off the credit line from the caption proper. A good spot to place a credit line is below the caption flush right. You can also place a credit line flush right between the picture and the caption if you do not have a headline over the caption.

Remember, the caption is the main type attraction. Identification of the picture source is secondary. The photographer's name and identity or the source, such as AP photo, are sufficient. If the photo is an old one from an archive, tell readers that in your credit line.

■ Description
(See also **Questions**)

Don't state the obvious. A caption should not say, *John Doe shakes hands with Ed Smith*, when it is obvious to the reader that Doe and Smith are shaking hands. Focus on what the picture can't tell the reader — why is Doe shaking Smith's hand and, perhaps, where?

But do explain questionable objects in the picture.

Picture editing is the best way to deal with this problem; crop out unrelated and distracting objects. But if such objects must be left in the photo, explain them. Good pictures, like good stories, should contain no clutter. So it follows that captions as well should not be cluttered with excess explanation.

This caption was under a multi-column picture of two people — one on the left in street clothes is obviously lecturing with emotion the one on the right, who is in a football uniform.

Former Philadelphia Eagles cornerback Herman Edwards (left) is best known for his Miracle at the Meadowlands, a miraculous last-minute touchdown he scored in 1978. His coaching internship with the Chiefs ends today.

The caption says, "Former Philadelphia Eagles cornerback Herman Edwards (left) is best known for his Miracle at the Meadowlands, a miraculous last-minute touchdown he scored in 1978. His coaching internship with the Chiefs ends today."

The picture probably was taken from the publication's library files to "dress up" the story on Edwards' ending his coaching internship. The picture has action — gesture, facial expression, body language — and two people. What's happening? Readers will not only wonder who the unidentified man on the right is, they also will be curious about what Edwards is doing, even though the action may not be current. If you show readers something, explain it.

But use common sense. A minor distraction that has no role in the picture's action need not be explained. For example, an ordinary picture on a wall in the background would not need explanation.

■ Groups

Try to avoid posed pictures of large groups staring into the camera. If you must, and many small-circulation publications feel obliged to publish group photos, use common sense in writing captions. Identify people left to right by rows. If there are too many people in the picture, perhaps you don't want to identify each person. In a small community, readers will know most of the people in the picture. If the picture is important (historic or relevant to news), then perhaps a diagram that numbers each person is needed. Create a package with the photo, a line drawing of the group in the photo with a number on each person's outline, and a numbered list of the people's names.

It helps caption writing if publications set guidelines for taking or accepting group photos. Photographers should have the caption in mind when setting up a group photo. Rows should be well-defined.

In unposed group photos in which people in the picture must be identified, use a simple guide to naming — left to right, clockwise, etc. Use common sense to determine whether identities are necessary. Obviously, in a riot scene, identity is not practical. In a small group waiting in line for tickets to a concert, names are practical, but not always necessary. In a large group in a ticket line, names are not practical. Think of the news value. If you publish a file picture of a group standing in line several years ago alongside a current picture of a few stragglers buying tickets for a similar event currently, it's not necessary to publish names. The purpose (news value) of the pictures is comparison, not who's in them.

■ Lead-ins and headlines
(See also Appearance)

Bold faced or capitalized words preceding the opening sentence of the caption accomplishes little. That graphic device is not attractive, it is often contrived, and it delays reader access to caption information. Bold facing the first few words of the first sentence is more practical as far as readability is concerned, but it adds nothing to appearance. A uniform caption of all one readable type face is more appealing. It has symmetry. A headline above the picture or between the picture and caption is a much more effective and attractive device. (See *The New York Times* example in the Mood section below.)

■ Mood

Try to pick up the mood of the picture. If the picture is light and entertaining, write the caption to fit the mood. But don't make light of tragic images.

This caption from *The New York Times* treats a serious incident lightly. The incident injured no one, but was unusual enough to inspire an unusual caption. The headline over the picture said, *What Next, Locusts?* The caption read:

In a spectacular accident in Manhattan yesterday, a century-old water main under Fifth Avenue ruptured, flooding streets and lobbies and gouging out a huge sinkhole that swallowed a car. The shifting asphalt broke a gas main and the gas ignited. No one was injured, but buildings were evacuated and subway service interrupted. The avenue between 19th and 21st Streets was expected to be closed for a week.

■ Mugs

The mug shot — head shot, or portrait — needs little explanation. It's generally used with a story to show readers a main character in the story. A name under the picture is sufficient. However, depending on the story, the identifying lines might include a title, a few words about the person's role in the story, a brief quotation, etc. But no more than a few lines. Identification with mugs, whether they are a half column, one column or multi-columns, should be brief and clear. When you have more to say about the person in the mug, write a separate story to package with the mug. Don't write long explanations in a mug-shot caption. A long block of type with no paragraphs is difficult to read.

Half-column mugs dropped in the text of a story look better when the caption is placed in white space next to the picture, filling out the column width. Running story type around a half-column picture creates an ugly segment of body type that is narrow and difficult to read, and the caption is squeezed into a narrow space. If you must use half-column mugs, give them an attractive display. Open up. You're not packing a suitcase.

Besides being a design problem, half-column pictures can cause production headaches. When pages were assembled manually, the small half-column pictures were frequently lost. A composing room foreman I worked with had little patience when half-column mugs didn't show up. He threatened to send pages to press with white space if the half-column picture did not show up by deadline, but few took him seriously — until a half-column white space appeared on a page.

At another newspaper, a missing half-column mug mysteriously turned up on several pages of the paper. The small picture, which was pasted in its proper place on a page, became unglued and adhered to the glass cover of the vacuum device that holds pages flat while they are photographed in the plate-making process. Every page photographed on that vacuum device for that edition included the same strange, tiny mug — in stories, ads, and in other pictures. We frantically searched to find all the pages infected by the "mug virus," and of course, several pages had to be remade for the rest of the press run.

■ No caption

Most pictures need a caption. However, there may be times when a picture tells a complete story, and only a few words of a headline are necessary. For example, a newspaper story about the glare of urban lights hiding all but the brightest stars in the night sky uses this display:

• A multi-column picture of the horizon at night. A planetarium is silhouetted on the horizon by the glare of urban lights.
• A reverse (white) headline in the dark sky at the top of the picture says, "Glow makes glimmer dimmer."
• No caption under the picture.
• A small drop head above the first column of the story (which is below the picture) says, "Starlight, once bright, missing in the sky at night."

No caption is necessary in this package. The picture and story are complete. There is nothing in the photo that needs explanation.

■ Obvious

Let the picture tell the story. Help the story with a terse caption if necessary, but don't tell readers what they can obviously see in the picture. This caption appeared under a picture of a church fire. The roof is ablaze, and fire is shooting from windows. The action is obvious. And a complete story on the fire is under the picture. A simple explanation is all that's needed. Instead, the caption writer includes not only details from the story but the work of the photographer.

The May United Methodist Church is captured in the above photo as a fire engulfs the roof of the church Saturday, Jan. 29. The two story structure was completely destroyed and included 24 memorial stained glass windows. Firefighters from May and North Lake Brownwood Fire Departments, along with Brownwood Fire Department, battled the blaze.

The May United Methodist Church is captured in the above photo as a fire engulfs the roof of the church Saturday, Jan. 29. The two story structure was completely destroyed and included 24 memorial stained glass windows. Firefighters from May and North Lake Brownwood Volunteer Fire Departments, along with Brownwood Fire Department, battled the blaze. (Photo by Dennis Hester)

No need to tell readers that the photo captures the fire. That is obvious. The only help the reader needs is identification — Fire destroyed May United Methodist Church Saturday. Save the rest for the story.

■ Parroting

Don't parrot lines from an accompanying story or the headline. Once is enough. Find a fresh approach for the caption. Make readers want to read the story. Here's an extreme parroting example.

The headline:

After 39 years, barber Foy Brown to cut loose

Story lead:

Foy Brown, 86, will pack away his scissors and clippers, then hang up his cape for the last time on February 25.

Caption for picture No. 1:

Foy Brown, 86, will retire on February 25. He has been cutting hair at Brown's Barber Shop on Halsell Street for the past 39 years.

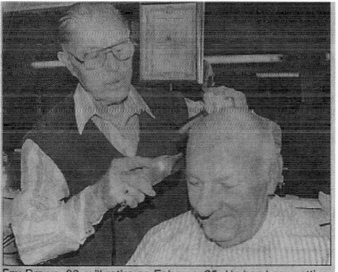

Foy Brown, 86, will retire on February 25. He has been cutting hair at Brown's Barber Shop on Halsell Street for the past 39 years.
— Indexfoto / Dorothy Clark

Barber Foy Brown, 86, will put his scissors and clippers away, then hang up his cape for the last time February 25. He has worked at the first chair in Brown's Barber Shop on Halsell Street since 1969.
- Indexfoto / Dorothy Clark

Caption for picture No. 2:

Barber Foy Brown, 86, will put his scissors and clippers away, then hang up his cape for the last time February 25. He has worked at the first chair in Brown's Barber Shop on Halsell Street since 1969.

Do you think readers will get the idea that Foy is 86,

he's been a barber for 39 years, and will retire February 25? And by the way, is *cut loose* a good choice of words for the headline?

■ Punctuation

Keep punctuation in captions to a minimum. Captions are meant to be read quickly. Apply standard punctuation rules to captions, but generally avoid parentheses. Parentheses are disruptive and make slow reading.

■ Questions

Captions should not create questions. They should answer them. If there are five people in a picture and you identify four, you create a question: Who is the other person? If what is happening in the picture is not obvious, explain it.

Franki Jo Jones has been selected for inclusion in Who's Who Among American Teachers for the second year in a row. She was recently recognized for 25 years of dedicated service to the students of Greenwood, and she was named VIP of the Year in 1996-97.

This caption ran below a photo of a man and a woman:

Franki Jo Jones has been selected for inclusion in Who's Who Among American Teachers for the second year in a row. She was recently recognized for 25 years of dedicated service to the students of Greenwood, and she was named VIP of the Year in 1996-97.

Question: Who's the guy on her left?

■ Tense

Generally use the present tense in captions, but do not use it incongruously. In describing the action in the picture — what is happening right now as the reader watches — the present tense is most often preferred.

However, you should not have a sentence that contains a past time and a present tense verb.

For example, you wouldn't write: "Councilman Harry Butts speaks yesterday at a rally of citizens who support removal of the ban on Main Street parking." The verb has to be *spoke*, the past tense, or *speaking*, the present participle. "Councilman Harry Butts, speaking yesterday at a rally . . . urged citizens to . . ." The present tense, *speaks*, does not agree with the time element, *yesterday*.

If you remove the time element, the present tense is appropriate: "Councilman Harry Butts speaks at a rally of citizens who support removal of the ban on Main Street parking."

Captions usually are written in the present tense, primarily because present tense provides a sense of immediacy, bringing the reader into the picture's action. Some news media styles, including that of The Associated Press, say that the first line of nearly all captions should be written in the present tense. Following sentences, usually adding background or supplementary information, may be in past, present, or future tense, according to the context. Here's an example of incorrect verb tense from an accident photo caption:

An early afternoon accident injures five people in Lumberton Saturday.

The verb must agree with the time. It should be *injured*, the past tense, because the accident happened in the past. The present tense can be used to describe past action if you do not include the time in the same sentence.

Here's an example in which the opening sentence has a present tense verb and the supplementary material in the second sentence is past:

Led by pilot Todd Hays of Texas, the USA-1 four-man bobsled team starts down the track. The sled took silver in Saturday's competition.

The action in this picture is obviously past, but the caption is in the present tense because the time is not mentioned:

U.S. Department of Transportation inspector Jeffrey Crow singles out a Mexican truck from the U.S. customs line for inspection at the World Trade Bridge in Laredo.

However, it is acceptable to use the past tense in that caption, even though the time is not in the sentence. Some newspapers have begun using the past tense in captions regardless of whether the time is mentioned. For example:

A mourner shot into the air as tens of thousands of Palestinians in the West Bank city of Nablus demonstrated during funeral processions for the eight victims of an Israeli missile strike on an office in Hamas.

The action is past and there is nothing wrong with using the past tense. The immediate access to news and information through broadcast media and the Internet makes immediacy in print captions seem unnecessary. Readers know the action happened in the past. The story accompanying the picture is written in the past tense, so why be different in the caption? Another newspaper, following the present-tense style, wrote the demonstration caption this way:

A mourner shoots in the air over Palestinians demonstrating during the funeral of eight people killed Tuesday in an Israeli missile attack on the offices of the militant group Hamas.

Present tense is acceptable. The time of the action is not mentioned. However, readers know the action is past, so why try to create immediacy?

Sometimes the present participle can be used to

describe past action:

> A Pakistani police officer escorting Ahmed Omar Sheikh to court Monday.

The writer in that passage is speaking to readers, describing what is happening in the picture — the officer is escorting. It's conversational and it's also a fragment; the caption writer in a sense is saying, "In this picture taken Monday, the officer is escorting . . ." A sentence fragment is acceptable when it is the only information in the caption or when it is the first sentence. If information follows the fragment, it should be written in complete sentences.

■ Wild or with story

Pictures with stories need minimal description. Pictures that stand alone need a bit more, but not much. A picture that is good enough to publish should tell a story. The caption should enhance that story. Generally, two sentences are all that is needed for a wild picture — one that has no story with it. Obviously, there will be times when two sentences will not do the job. Use common sense.

Keep captions brief. If you find you need more background or supplementary information, put it in a separate story or display with the picture (See also Brevity). One sentence, and sometimes a sentence fragment, normally is sufficient for a caption with a story. Do not repeat sizable segments of information from the story. You want to draw readers to the story. Describe the picture and tease the reader into the story. Picture-caption displays, like headlines, should invite readers to go beyond — to venture into the story.

The argument that you want to provide readers who are in a hurry enough information so that they do not have to read the story is contrary to the purpose of the medium. You want readers to READ your publication. Do everything you can to make them read it. Inviting headlines and captions are part of your lure.

■ Wordy

Be frugal with words. Style rules that demand captions fill a certain amount of space don't help readers. A caption should contain enough words to help the reader see the picture as the photographer saw it. Padding to fill out a certain number of lines or to balance the depth of two columns does not help the reader. A publication should adopt flexible guidelines for captions and toss out rigid style rules that make captions unattractive and difficult to read. Remember the proverb: *One picture is worth more than ten thousand words*. A few words of explanation should be sufficient.

But don't go too far in your explanation. Identify people and objects only when necessary. Long lists of people or objects make dull reading. Captions should be short and snappy. When it is necessary to identify people in a picture, provide help for the reader — *left, right, first row*, etc.

Also remember that a caption helps the picture. If there's a story beyond the picture, tell it separately. Captions should not take the place of stories. This caption, which was tucked into a one column armpit of two action pictures, goes far beyond helping the pictures. It's a separate story. It's also difficult to read because it lacks paragraphs. Explain the pictures in the caption, and tell about the Lady Tigers' coming basketball season in a separate story.

Terrell junior point guard Stephanie Pierson (pictured above) returns for her third season as a starter for the Lady Tigers. Pierson was District 14-4A Newcomer of The Year as a freshman and was named all-district in District 16-4A as a sophomore. Senior guard Ariel Holmes (shown at right) finished in the top five in the area in three-point shooting last year among both Class 4A and 5A players. Holmes is also a three-year starter for the Lady Tigers. She was second team all-district as a sophomore and was a first team all-district selection last year. Terrell coach Todd Evans said the Lady Tigers' fortunes in the district race will depend on how well Pierson and Holmes perform as well as how healthy Terrell's players remain.

Exercises

Headline writing

1. Using the same method shown in Chapter 2, rewrite the British theater headline as a two-line headline with a count of about 30 units per line. Write it first as a serious "looker" head and then as a light "hooker" headline. Use the same number of lines and unit count for both headlines.

2. Find in a publication you read regularly a headline written in the passive voice. Does it work? If it does, explain why. If not, explain why and rewrite it as an active-voice headline. Then find a poor active-voice headline and improve it by rewriting it as a passive headline.

3. Look at several publications — newspapers, magazines, brochures, posters, etc. — and critique the headline type style. Can you improve the appearance of the headlines by changing the type face, size, or position? If so, how? If not, why? Be specific.

4. In any publication, find a headline that uses a colon or a dash for attribution. Rewrite it without the colon or dash, using the same style, space, and count as the original.

5. Find a good newspaper feature story headline that has both a subject and a verb. Rewrite the headline as a label. Change the headline specs to suit your new headline. Explain the steps you took to write the new headline.

6. Search several publications to find a story suitable for a question headline. Then write a question head. Explain why the question headline is better for that story than the original headline.

7. In any publication, find a story that's suitable for a headline using onomatopoeia. Write a new head using onomatopoeia.

8. Find a headline that you can improve by using a pun, metaphor, or rhyme. Rewrite it using one of those devices. Explain how your device improved the headline.

9. Look through a newspaper for split headlines. Find five and rewrite them without splitting.

10. Find in any publication 10 headline words that can be used as two or more parts of speech (e.g. nouns as verbs, verbs as adjectives, etc.). Give an example of how each could be used to produce two-faced heads.

Caption writing

1. Find a wordy caption in any publication and condense it to one or two reasonable-length sentences.

2. How would you improve the caption on Page 76 titled "DEPUTIES HONORED"? Be specific in explaining your changes. Rewrite it.

3. Repair the caption for the Terrell Lady Tiger picture on Page 91. It is being published with a story. Rewrite it in two sentences if possible.

4. In any publication, find a caption that does not capture the mood of its picture. Explain why and rewrite the caption to improve it. Now find a picture that has a good "mood" caption and explain why it works.

5. How would you handle the Foy Brown layout mentioned on Page 85? Be specific and address not only the captions but the display of the story and two pictures.

Acknowledgments

The headline portion of this book is the result of years of collecting. Many of the examples came from friends, colleagues, students and readers who over the years have given me published headlines that made them laugh, insulted their intelligence, or were pretty near perfect. Others my wife, Paula, and I gathered from publications across the country. Still others came from publications such as *CJR* and *AJR*.

I'm indebted to John B. Bremner, the author of *HTK*, a marvelous little book on headline writing that was published many years ago and has been a valuable guide to writing good headlines and teaching headline writing. My thanks also to Richard Lederer whose many books on language and words provided not only entertainment but fueled my love of words, particularly strong, short words — the words that make good headlines.

My deskmates at *The Milwaukee Journal* during the '60s deserve special thanks for their help in writing headlines. Thanks too to the headline and caption writers of *The New York Times, The Wall Street Journal,* and *The Dallas Morning News* for some of the good examples I've cited. And thanks to The Associated Press and *The Wall Street Journal* for the theater and doughnut stories I used to illustrate headline development in Chapter 2.

Many of the captions in this book are examples collected at editing seminars I've conducted for various organizations and newspapers. Special thanks to The Assciated Press, *The Kansas City Star*, the *Rising Star*, Rising Star, Texas, the *Greenwood Ranger*, Midland, Texas, and *The Dallas Morning News*, for the pictures reprinted in the caption segment.

Most of all, I'm thankful for such a talented and loving wife who edits with severity and care all my work, and whose love of the English language inspires me daily. She's not only my partner in life, but also my partner in writing.

Index